Amsterdam

Amsterdam

By Ryan Levitt

Thomas
Cook
Publishing

The
Pink Paper

Published by Thomas Cook Publishing
PO Box 227
The Thomas Cook Business Park
Coningsby Road
Peterborough
PE3 8XX

E-mail: books@thomascook.com

ISBN: 1841571 601

Text © 2002 Thomas Cook Publishing
Maps © 2002 Thomas Cook Publishing

For Thomas Cook Publishing
Managing Director: Kevin Fitzgerald
Publisher: Donald Greig
Commissioning Editor: Deborah Parker
Editor: Sarah Hudson
Proofreader: Jan Wiltshire

For Pink Paper
General Manager: David Bridle
Publishing Manager: Mike Ross
Editor: Steve Anthony
Additional picture research: Claire Benjamin

Design: Studio 183 and Grassverge
Layout: Studio 183, Peterborough
Cover Design: Studio 183 and Grassverge
Cover Artwork: Steve Clarke, Studio 183

City maps drawn by: Steve Munns
Transport maps: Transport Cartographic Service

Scanning: Dale Carrington, Chronos Publishing; David Bruce Graphics

Printed and bound in Spain by: Artes Gráficas Elkar, Loiu, Spain

Written and researched by Ryan Levitt
Photography: Gavin Harrison

Additional photography:
Amsterdam Tourist Office (page 104 and 118)
Amanda Lehner (page 13, Erotic Musuem page 14; 21; 22; 23; 25; 30; 31; 41; 45; 46; 48;
50; 53; 55; 57; 58; 60; 65; 78; 80; 81; 83; 87; 101; 108; 109; 120 and 124.
Black Tulip (page 122)
Gaze (page 105)
Scott Nunn: (page 144)
Tropenmuseum (pages 66 and 67)
Queercompany.com (page 144)

Cover photographs: Gavin Harrison; Scott Nunn

Contents

CONTENTS

Prices throughout this book are given
in guilders as many of their euro
values had not been finalised at the
time of going to press.
1 € = f 2.20

My kind of town...

Why do I love the Netherlands? Is it for its picturesque canals? The endless fields of tulips? The welcoming attitude towards homosexuality, or perhaps for its notorious wild side?

It's all of these things, and more. Travels around the globe have brought me to countless cities, five continents, tropical islands and forbidden palaces, yet nothing can quite compare to the excitement and wonder the city of Amsterdam holds for me every time I explore its cobblestoned streets.

When I first visited Amsterdam, I thought of it as the place to go for wild weed, summers of sin and sultry nights of fun and frivolity. Age and education have opened my eyes to the other side of the city; a walkable maze of streets dripping with history, art treasures, stellar shopping and cosy canals.

But you can't write about this self-proclaimed 'gayest city of Europe' without injecting an element of whimsy and mystery to match the characteristics of its residents. As a travel writer specialising in gay travel destinations, I have seen my work printed in a number of publications including *Fluid*, *Attitude*, the *Pink Paper* and *Out & About*. I suppose coming from a suburban Canadian background may have something to do with my desire to explore the world – and Amsterdam is about as far away ideologically as you can get.

Sure, you've got the dope and the dykes, but you also have one of the most socially aware societies in the world. It's a mindset that is both thought-provoking and enticing.

I will always hold a place in my heart for this magic metropolis made for those on a queer quest. So pack your bags and get your clogs polished because you're about to embark on the gay adventure of a lifetime. Just don't fall into any of the canals (it's easier than you think).

Plenty of canals to explore

Out in Amsterdam

It used to be said that the Dutch were only known for a few things: windmills, tulips, wooden clogs and cheese. Today, while all of the above are still associated with Dutch heritage and culture, it is for its relaxed and tolerant society that the Netherlands is now most highly regarded.

The forward-thinking Dutch originally took homosexuality off the law books in 1811. You could blame Holland's nautical tradition and proliferation of sea-bound young sailors for this decision to make same-sex sexuality legal, but in reality it is the Dutch people's laissez-faire attitude to life in general that tends to win over the lawmakers.

This early acceptance of homosexuality has led Amsterdam to create what is probably the world's only memorial to persecuted homosexuals from across the globe. Honouring gay pasts and futures, the Homo-monument, designed by Karin Daan, features three triangles of pink granite that together form one larger triangle jutting out into the waters of the Keizersgracht.

The Homomonument is the centre of the action on Queen's Day, World War II Memorial Day (May 4) and World AIDS Day (December 1), when a variety of tributes and concerts are planned to honour the dead and celebrate the living. The Homomonument is adjacent to the Westerkerk near Anne Frank's house.

In Amsterdam, homosexuals are treated like any other human being; with dignity, respect and a degree of aloofness. Locals won't stare at you if you decide to hold hands or kiss your partner in public. They've pretty much seen, if not done it all.

For visitors from less tolerant nations, this wide-open policy of 'live and let live' can be a bit daunting. Tourists often complain that the gay community atmosphere found in many international cities does not exist in Amsterdam. However, those who know the city well will argue that a gay community doesn't exist because members of Dutch gay society don't need to band together to fight for anything any more.

Being gay doesn't make you special in Amsterdam. You can get married and have kids just like any straight person. Most gay Amsterdammers miss having any form of unique status, lamenting a loss of culture and identity in their search for equality. But, due to their non-confrontational manner, the gay Dutch won't make any noise about it, preferring instead to politely voice their grievances over a glass of foamy beer.

Always a leader in terms of gay rights, gay marriage is just the latest in a long string of laws

At the tea dance

created to equalise rights between gays and straights since the age of consent was made consistent at 16 years old in 1971. Legalised in 2000, the Netherlands celebrated its first gay marriages in Rotterdam in early 2001, to great media interest. But if you ask most local gays, they'll probably tell you that they never plan on getting married, regardless of the changes to the law books.

The open nature of Dutch society allows travellers to explore some of the more liberal aspects of gay sexuality, with darkrooms, prostitution and SM practices legal for one and all. Darkrooms are subject to strict health regulations, with safer sex material visibly displayed in every corner and condoms and lube readily available to all.

The Dutch government takes a very enlightened view towards combating the spread of HIV, avoiding the non-confrontational approach many less tolerant governments have taken to teach HIV prevention. HIV campaigns are explicit, informative and they get right to the point. Those who don't practise safer sex won't be tolerated in Dutch sex establishments, and you may quickly find yourself on the street if you

approach anyone with thoughts of latex-free sex.

Legal male prostitution, like its straight counterpart found in the red-light district, is available, with escort services, hustler bars and male brothels advertised in almost every gay publication. All prostitutes are required to go through health check-ups every three months, and safe sex is a mandatory requirement for all who decide to visit one.

The gay media is well established in the city, with a selection of Dutch and bilingual publications on offer to visitors.

One of the best places to pick up reading materials is at the Pink Point of Presence, a volunteer-based booth located near the Homomonument that specialises in providing tourist information to gay travellers. Depending on the season, the booth is usually open April to October daily from noon to 6pm.

The best listings and event details for English speakers can be found in the *Gay News*, free at most gay establishments. Don't get suckered into buying a copy at any of the magazine shops or bookstores in the city, as you'll save yourself the cost simply by walking into any gay bar. Other publications to look out for include the hip style bible *Squeeze* (Dutch only), the new art and design booklet *Butt* (bilingual), *De Gay Krant* (Dutch) and the major local gay and lesbian radio station MVS. English-language programmes are offered on MVS every Sunday evening.

HIV-positive travellers will find any visit to the Netherlands extremely pleasant. Unlike many other nations, there are no

Warmoesstraat – heart of the leather community

restrictions to travel and there is little stigma attached to those who carry the disease. The Schorer Foundation is a useful resource for HIV-positive tourists interested in planning a trip to the city, offering a number of services to gay men with HIV and AIDS.

In addition to psychosocial counselling and an offsite HIV clinic, the Foundation also has a helpdesk number (tel: 31 20 662 42 06) and a volunteer project for those in need of short-term practical assistance.

One of the odd things you may notice about gay establishments is the number of straights that own them. While other cities look at straight ownership as exploitation of the community, Amsterdammers look at all businesses as viable financial enterprises. Straights are

readily accepted into gay society, with the exception of the leather and rubber scenes.

Some of the choosier clubs may have a strict gay-only door policy, but the inevitable 'fag hag' usually manages to slip her way past the burly bouncers.

Other than the occasional pickpocket, safety isn't really a problem for tourists in Amsterdam. Gay hate-crimes are almost unheard of and the police even have their own gay division and specially appointed officers to assist you if you get into trouble.

So kick back in the coffeeshops, discover the dungeons, cruise the canals and dance till you drop 'cause Amsterdam is sure to transform your view about what a gay holiday can be all about. You may never want to leave.

Stepping Out

Amsterdam is a treasure trove of sightseeing delights, each representing different aspects of the culture, tradition and history for which the city is renowned. Many of the top tourist traps include a gay angle in their exhibits, usually involving a dash of whimsy that only an Amsterdammer could inject. While a traveller could spend weeks exploring the canals and pathways of Amsterdam, my top unmissable sights are as follows.

My Top Sights

Albert Cuypmarkt

ℹ️ At the Junction of Albert Cuypstraat and Ferdinand Bolstraat ⏱️ 9.30am–5pm Mon–Sat; Closed Sun 🚊 Trams 4, 16, 24, 25 💶 Free

The bustling Cuypmarkt

Amsterdam's biggest market, the Albert Cuypmarkt, is a massive, sprawling mess of clothes, food, art supplies and DIY finds located in the heart of one of Amsterdam's hippest neighbourhoods, The Pijp. With Amsterdam's densest population of gay residents, The Pijp is a great slice of authentic Dutch life, with Albert Cuypmarkt acting as the centre of the action. Leave your credit cards at home though, as it's cash you'll need for the bargains. (See p. 55)

Amsterdams Historisch Museum

ℹ️ Kalverstraat 92 📞 523-1822 www.ahm.nl ⏱️ 10am–5pm Mon–Fri; 11am–5pm Sat & Sun 🚊 Trams 1, 2, 4, 5, 9, 14, 16, 20, 24, 25 💶 f12. No credit cards

STEPPING OUT

Museums that dictate a city's history tend to be a bore, but the Amsterdams Historisch Museum is a real eye-opener. Beginning with a computer map that reveals the growth of the city before your eyes, the museum leads you from Amsterdam's early days as a stretch of swampland right through to the modern day.

The highlight comes at the end of the tour where a salute to Amsterdam's gay life has been painstakingly put together in the form of a detailed reconstruction of one of the city's first gay establishments, Cafe Maandje, featuring a very entertaining interview with the original Dutch Dyke on a Bike, Bet van Beeren. (*See p. 38*)

Anne Frankhuis

ℹ Prinsengracht 263 📞 556-7100
www.annefrank.nl ⏰ Jan–Mar, Sep–Dec 9am–7pm
daily; Apr–Aug 9am–9pm daily; Closed Yom Kippur;
entrance shuts half an hour before closing time
🚊 Tram 13, 14, 17, 20 💲 fl12.50. No credit cards

Anne Frankhuis

A powerful symbol of wartime Amsterdam and the plight of European Jewry under the heavy hand of Hitler, the Anne Frankhuis is a stunning memorial to the courageous German girl whose belief in humanity touched the world. Diary excerpts and photographs outline the cramped conditions of the Secret Annexe, with a large room at the end of the tour dedicated to the struggle for freedom, democracy and human rights. Unfortunately lacking is any reference to the sufferings of the gay community. Despite this omission, the house is still one of Amsterdam's best sights and the long queue permanently snaking around its edges is a testament to that fact. Make sure to get there early otherwise you'll be waiting behind endless groups of screaming Dutch schoolchildren. (*See p. 30*)

Come on in . . .

Erotic Museum

ℹ Oudezijds Achterburgwal 54
📞 624-7303
⏰ 11am–1am Mon, Thu & Sun;
11am–2am Fri & Sat; Closed Tue & Wed
🚊 Trams 4, 9, 16, 20, 24, 25
💲 f5. No credit cards

Tasteless, poorly maintained, filled with junk and cashing very obviously on the rather less-than-salubrious neighbourhood it finds itself in, the Erotic Museum is a laughable collection of all things related to sex. Gay objects are non-existent, but the museum is a hysterical and highly appropriate introduction to the world of Amsterdam's Red-Light District.

Bring plenty of irony and check your brain at the door. (*See p. 46*)

Heineken Brewery

ⓘ Stadhouderskade 78

☎ 523-9239/recorded information 523-9666

☀ Tours 9.30am & 11am Mon–Fri; Closed Sat & Sun

🚊 Trams 6, 7, 10, 16, 20, 24

🎟 f2. Credit cards: AmEx, M, V

Refreshes the parts . . .

Closed for most of 2001 due to major refurbishments, no one really knows exactly what the Heineken Brewery (*Brouwerij*) has in store when it reopens, least of all its employees. No longer an operating brewery, the tour is essentially a huge advertising campaign designed to drill the idea that 'Heineken is Good!' into the minds of unsuspecting tourists. Ignore the historical blather and prepare yourself for the all-you-can-drink gorge fest that awaits you at the other end. (*See p. 55*)

Homomonument

ⓘ Westermarkt

☀ All year. Special Events on Queen's Day (30 April), Liberation Day (4 May) and World AIDS Day (1 Dec)

🚊 Tram 13, 14, 17

🎟 Free

Unveiled in 1987, the Homomonument is the world's only monument to gay men and lesbians who have been persecuted and oppressed because of their sexuality. The monument, designed by Karin Daan, is made up of three triangles of pink granite, each representing a different aspect of the struggle for gay acceptance.

Windy days should be avoided, however, as the stream of pee from the nearby pissoir sometimes manages to add its own special touch to the memorial. (*See p. 31*)

A monument to persecution

Rijksmuseum

ⓘ Stadhouderskade 42
📞 674-7047
www.rijksmuseum.nl
🕐 10am–5pm daily
🚊 Trams 2, 5, 6, 7, 10, 20
💳 f15. Credit cards: V

A collection of masterpieces

The largest collection of art in the Netherlands, the Rijksmuseum could easily fill a day for even the most philistine of travellers.

Strong on Dutch Masters, decorative arts and Asian treasures, the Rijksmuseum is definitely the place to go if dark oil portraits and still lifes of rotting fruit are your thing.

Rembrandt's *Night Watch*, widely considered to be the masterpiece of the collection, is located in this, the crown jewel of Amsterdam's art galleries.

Get your elbows at the ready to move the gaping, dumbstruck tourists out of the way for a clear view and prepare to be awestruck. (*See p. 58*)

Stedelijk Museum of Modern Art

ⓘ Paulus Potterstraat 13
📞 573-2737 www.stedelijk.nl
🕐 11am–5pm daily **🚊** Trams 2, 5, 6, 7, 10, 20
💳 f10. No credit cards. Gift shop accepts AmEx, M, V

Showcase of modern art

Number two of Amsterdam's three major art museums, the Stedelijk is the centre for modern art in the city, with an impressive collection including works by Matisse, Picasso, Chagall, De Kooning, Lichtenstein, Stella and Warhol.

Not the most architecturally beautiful of Amsterdam's buildings, the museum tries to fuse together a generic example of neo-Renaissance with an unsightly 'new' wing built in 1954.

Inside, however, the art is well presented, with light, airy rooms providing an apt showcase for the exciting temporary and permanent collections. (*See p. 58*)

Van Gogh Museum

ℹ️ Paulus Potterstraat 7
📞 570-5200 www.vangoghmuseum.nl
🕐 10am–6pm daily
🚃 Trams 2, 3, 5, 12, 16, 20
💳 f15.50. Credit cards: M, V

To the Van Gogh Museum, and the most impressive collection in the world dedicated to the works of the much-misunderstood Dutchman.

More than 700 of his drawings and paintings are amassed here in a collection which manages to inspire, even when seen from behind the backs of the unruly tour groups.

Works by other artists of the Impressionist period are also exhibited in an effort to lend a bit of perspective. But you just can't help but be impressed by the guy. (See p. 58)

This way . . .

Vondelpark

ℹ️ Vondelpark 🕐 24 hours daily 🚃 Trams 1, 2, 3, 5, 6, 12, 20 💳 Free

The largest park in the city, Vondelpark is a combination of hippie hangout, skateboarder heaven, and urban rest stop for those in need of a rural respite. On sunny days and weekends, the park is taken over by the sound of bongo-playing, the scent of dope and the sight of teenage hippies desperately trying to revive a decade long since dead.

Friday nights should be avoided unless you want to take your life into your own hands by playing dodgems with the local rollerbladers.

After dark, the Vondelpark takes on a completely different character, with gentlemen often to be found wandering the paths in search of exercise of a quite different nature. (See p. 59)

Vondelpark offers varied attractions

Amsterdam boats, buildings and canals

Around Town

Amsterdam is a very compact city and combining neighbourhoods does not present a problem. Geographically, the major canals act as obvious neighbourhood dividers, spreading circularly around the city from Centraal Station. Fans of the Golden Age should stick to the art of the Museum Quarter and the architecture of the Northern Canals, while those on a bender will probably prefer Grachtengordel East and the Red-Light District.

Grachtengordel East

Not really a neighbourhood for sightseeing, Grachtengordel East is the less scenic section of the canal district known as the Grachtengordel. The area focuses more on stuff to do rather than stuff to see – and what a lot of stuff to do there is! Three of the city's four main gay 'villages' are located in this easily walkable part of town, each one catering to a completely different clientele and age range. Shopping on the Leidsestraat is another bonus, with branches of all the big chain shops located along this central artery.

But history is not completely thrown aside. The Leidseplein has been known for centuries as a gathering place for artists, protesters and pickpockets, while examples of 17th-century life and architecture can be found in museums dotted around the district. For the perfect encapsulation of all things Grachtengordel, head over to the Backstage Café, a shop/bar/gay history venue that combines everything in which the area specialises.

A DAY OUT

Many consider the Leidseplein to be the centre of Amsterdam. Intrigue, espionage and football hooligans have flocked here at various points during the plaza's history, making the area a hotbed of action. Begin your day late, as the Grachtengordel is known more for its nightlife than its daytime attractions.

Shopaholics will want to roam the Leidsestraat, which is always cluttered with crowds of locals, while label queens should head directly to Metz & Co to try on all the latest collections. While you won't pick up any deals outside of the usual sale periods, it's nice to dream.

Grachtengordel East

Leidseplein

Crossing the Leidsestraat halfway on its journey to the Singel is the Kerkstraat. Home to one of Amsterdam's four gay 'villages', the Kerkstraat is a down-to-earth place, combining a few leather bars with scattered speciality shops to create a kind of poor man's pink community.

Stylish lads and lasses should continue on, however, to the coolest gay strip in town, the Reguliersdwarsstraat. Don't worry about trying to pronounce the name of the street, even the Dutch have difficulty. If you need a break, you'll certainly get one by stopping off at Amsterdam's only gay coffeeshop, the Otherside. The steps outside the place get packed with weeded wonders, cruising both you and the quality of the latest dope delivery to pass the Otherside's back door.

Bars on the Reguliersdwarsstraat are a dime a dozen. All of them boast gorgeous bartenders, though none of them will take any notice of you unless your wallet is bulging. Soho and Havana are the usual hotspots of choice.

Those interested in the macabre might want to make a slight detour to the Torture Museum on Singel, while others who prefer to see nice, pretty things might prefer the tons of tulips available at the Bloemenmarkt. If you're feeling out of touch, technical types should drop into the internet café Easyeverything, on the Reguliersbreestraat as you walk towards the Rembrandtplein. It's often regarded as the best pick-up spot in town.

The cafés around the Rembrandtplein provide ample opportunities to rest your aching feet, with many offering gay-specific environments. Most of the gay bars open around 4pm, so you may have to do a little backtracking later in the day if you've arrived too early.

You could stop now, but a southern journey from the Rembrandtplein will take you to the fab café/restaurant, the Backstage Café. While it does take you away from the action, I cannot recommend this hilarious detour enough. Leave lots of time for flattery and fortune telling!

Rembrandtplein

Out to Lunch

Options aplenty line the streets of Grachtengordel East for dedicated followers of fusion. The hottest restaurant in town is easily **Inez IPSC**. Artsy types adore this place, designed by Peter Giele, who was one of the artistic minds behind the legendary gay nightclub, the Roxy. For an Amsterdam history lesson while you're eating then pop into **'t Swarte Schaep** for a glimpse of the 300-year-old building in which it's housed. Intrigue presents itself at the **Cafe Americain**, once home to the wedding reception of famous spy Mata Hari, while the café **Downtown** and the South African supper centre **Pygmalion** cater decidedly to a gay male clientele.

CAFE AMERICAIN

 Leidseplein 97
 624-5322
www.interconti.com/
netherlands/amsterdam
/dining_amsame.html

 7am– 1am daily
(non-guests are
welcome from 10am
onwards)

 Credit cards:
AmEx, M, V

DOWNTOWN

 Reguliersdwars-
straat 31
 622-9958
 10am– 7pm daily

 No credit cards

INEZ IPSC

 Amstel 2
 639-2899
 noon–3pm,
7–11.30pm daily

 Credit cards: M, V

PYGMALION

 Nieuwe
Spiegelstraat 5A
 420-7022
 11am– 3pm Mon;
11am–10pm Tue–Sun

 Credit cards:
AmEx, M, V

'T SWARTE SCHAEP

 Korte
Leidsedwarsstraat 24
 622-3021
 noon–11pm daily

 Credit cards:
AmEx, M, V

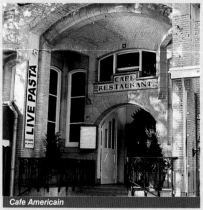

Cafe Americain

Bloemenmarkt

OUTLINES

BLOEMENMARKT

🛈 Along the Singel between Muntplein and Koningsplein 🕙 9am–5pm Mon–Sat; Closed Sun 🚊 Trams 1, 2, 4, 5, 9, 14, 16, 20, 24, 25 💶 Free

If you want tulips, do they have tulips! Big tulips, little tulips, red tulips, yellow tulips, tulip bulbs, tulip-growing food. It's bloomin' lovely. But just make sure you check your local import laws on flora before you make any bulk bulb buys.

HET KATTENKABINET

🛈 Herengracht 497 📞 626-5378 🕙 10am–2pm Mon–Fri; 1–5pm Sat–Sun 🚊 Trams 4, 9, 14, 16, 20, 24, 25 💶 f10. No credit cards

It's pussy galore at this freaky little museum dedicated to the world of the cat. Paintings, drawings and statues combine to illuminate the beauty and joy of this 'friendliest' of animals. Don't say anything bad about feline critters while you're anywhere near the place' though. The

owner might scratch your eyes out.

KERKSTRAAT

🚊 Trams 1, 2, 5, 16, 24, 25

If the three gay villages south of the Amstel were to be divided up into age groups, then the Kerkstraat would definitely be the one for retirees. Relaxed and casual, there is a decidedly more mature feel to the venues here. Beginning with the casual and campy leather bar De Spijker, a short trek east will take you past the Cosmo Bar, Amistad

AROUND TOWN

Hotel, The Golden Bear, Camp Café, Thermos Night Sauna and the Bronx Sex Shop. Like most other streets that rely on the bar trade, things don't really pick up until well into the evening.

MAGEREBRUG

ⓘ Linking Kerkstraat with Nieuwe Kerkstraat over the Amstel **ⓧ** All year **ⓜ** Tram 4

A monument to laziness, this one. Two sisters who lived on opposite sides of the Amstel River built the famous 'Skinny Bridge' or Magerebrug in the 17th century. Still in operation today, the bridge is made of wood and has to be continually repaired. Boats requiring access must open it by hand whenever passing. And all for a couple of girls who didn't like the long walk.

MAX EUWE CENTRUM

ⓘ Max Euweplein 30A
ⓒ 625–7017
www.maxeuwe.nl
ⓧ 10.30am–4pm Mon–Fri; Closed Sat & Sun
ⓜ Trams 1, 2, 5, 6, 7, 10
ⓥ Free

Chess fans will drop their knickers at the sight of this centre dedicated to the sport of 'queens'. The library and artefacts celebrate the game and the legacy of the only Dutch chess world champion, Max Euwe. There are loads of opportunities to get drawn into a game.

MUSEUM VAN LOON

ⓘ Keizersgracht 672
ⓒ 624-5255
www.musvanloon.box.nl
ⓧ 11am–5pm Mon, Fri–Sun; Closed Tue–Thu
ⓜ Trams 16, 24, 25
ⓥ f7.50. Credit cards: AmEx, MC, V

A restored canal house from the mid-18th century, the Museum van Loon illustrates what life would have been like if you were a posh canal resident during the days of Amsterdam's Golden Age. The interiors have changed little from that heyday, but it's a fact that one of Rembrandt's pupils, Ferdinand Bol, originally owned the house that gives this residence its noble seal of approval.

MUSEUM WILLET-HOLTHUYSEN

ⓘ Herengracht 605
ⓒ 523-1870
ⓧ 10am– 5pm Mon–Fri; 11am–5pm Sat & Sun
ⓜ Trams 4, 9, 14, 20
ⓥ f8. No credit cards

Another reconstructed 17th-century mansion, with furnishings from the 18th and 19th centuries, following the tastes of the family who bought the house in 1850. Whilst this place is worth a look due to the careful reconstructions and well-documented English translations, a visit should only be undertaken by those with strong interests in antiques and history. Go instead to the Rembrandthuis if you're short on time and shorter on money.

REGULIERSDWARS-STRAAT

ⓧ All year **ⓜ** Trams 1, 2, 5, 16, 24, 25

Muscle boys, scene queens and media whores flock to this street specialising in overpriced drinks and testosterone. Perfect is the only word to describe the clientele, the bar staff and the parties that go on late into the night in this gay scene centre. Sadly, perfect is not the word to describe the levels of service you'll find. Judging by the amount of time the staff spend on the phone, you'd be better off calling your orders in. Top venues include Havana, Soho, Downtown, Exit and the Otherside. Drinks are expensive. On Queen's Day the entire street lets loose for the party of a lifetime.

REMBRANDTPLEIN

☿ All year

🚊 Trams 4, 9, 14, 20

The streets around the Rembrandtplein offer those in search of refreshment a wide range of drinking establishments. Everything from hustler bars to Dutch singalong taverns to the legendary club iT pack into the alleys surrounding the historic square. The best thing to do to discover the area is to pub crawl from bar to bar. Each one has its own particular clientele and they'll all try and make you welcome. Older men might prefer the down home feel of the Amstel Taveerne, while younger guys should check out any of the holes-in-the-wall on the Halvemaanstreeg. But, if it's a dollop of the past combined with the disco of the present you crave, then it should be your final destination.

TORTURE MUSEUM

ℹ Singel 449 ☎ 320-6642 ☿ 10am–11pm daily 🚊 Trams 1, 2, 5 💰 f12. No credit cards

Sorry to disappoint anyone who thinks this might be an SM nightclub, but it is actually a collection of medieval devices of suffering. Everything from iron maidens to racks are on display in a dank, atmospheric basement designed to heighten the tension. But if you can handle a ghost train, you can handle this.

Museum van Loon

The Jordaan and Northern Canals

The Jordaan and Northern Canals (Grachtengordel West)

The Jordaan has always had an eclectic past. Once a neighbourhood built by victims of religious persecution, the small homes and high density that are characteristic of the district have now transformed it into the dwelling of choice for artists, students and those looking for the perfect pad in a funky part of town. The last decade has seen the mobilisation of killer-gentrifying yuppies as they attack the DIY stores with a vengeance. Let the battle of the charming split-level loft conversion commence.

Contrary to the Jordaan's proud community of working-class spirits and house-proud Hausfraus, the Grachtengordel (or Northern Canals) is the neighbourhood choice for the elite and elegant. Amsterdam's nouveau riche are charmed by the area's wide canals lined with leafy trees and beautiful homes dating back to the city's Golden Age. You will be, too.

Depending on when you're going, you might want to bring earplugs when wandering the placid pathways of the area. You'll need them to block out the constant hammering as construction workers endeavour to bring the various canal houses up to their completely remodelled splendour.

A DAY OUT

The old saying is that if you can hear the bells of the Westerkerk, then you're in the Jordaan. The geographic centre of the city's most idiosyncratic neighbourhood, it's also the best place to begin your day. Some of the best views of the city can be had from the top of the ancient church's tower, which also acts as a landmark if you get lost.

Outside the church, the Westermarkt plaza holds a number of attractions for the gay visitor, including the Homomonument and the Pink Point of Presence, a volunteer-run tourist information centre specialising in all things gay. It's a great resource for those on a queer quest, with staffers knowing all the best places to go, see, club and sup.

In order to avoid the endless crowds, the next stop should be Amsterdam's most poignant memorial museum, the Anne Frankhuis. The site of the last residence of Anne Frank, the house displays excerpts from her diary and photographs to describe her last days as she battled for life in the Secret Annexe. Check out the statue of Anne Frank at the corner

The Jordaan and Northern Canals

of the Westermarkt and Prinsengracht to see a true symbol of the heart of Amsterdam.

The Jordaan is not known for its sights. Rather, it is more of a multi-faceted residential neighbourhood combining some elegant homes with quirky shopping options. The district is made to be stumbled around rather than 'done'. Areas of interest to gay travellers include the home of the COC, Rozenstraat, the indoor antique markets of Rommelmarkt and Looier, the jumble sales of the Noordermarkt and the Rozengracht for its heady mix of brash boutiques and kitsch cafés.

More picturesque in a 'God, I could live like this!' sort of way are the Northern Canals. Heavy on law firms and accountancy offices, the Prinsengracht, Keizersgracht and Herengracht provide some of the most stunning canal views of the city. Watch your step as you're mesmerised by the boat traffic, as there are few barriers between you and a cold plunge into the inky depths.

An appropriate museum to check out is the Woonbootmuseum. An actual houseboat that shows what life is like on the numerous watery homes still used by many of the city's residents.

If you need a break, shoot down any of the streets that cross the main canals for a bit of light shopping or dining. Intimate is the name of the game for all the storefronts in the area, with bigger bonanzas found at the northern end of the canals on Haarlemmerstraat.

A typical building with a splash of colour

Out to Lunch

It's Dutch Treat in the restaurants and cafés of the Jordaan and Grachtengordel West. **Gary's Muffins** is a great way to begin the day with their organic and wholesome selection of freshly-baked muffins and bagels. A branch on the Reguliersdwarsstraat is a late-night hit with the gay crowd, while the outlet in this neighbourhood caters to the early-risers. If you prefer hash with your mash, give **Barney's** a try. You'll certainly get a case of the munchies just by walking into the ever-smoky dining area. Dutch pancakes with a wide variety of fillings can be found at the ever-popular **Pancake Bakery**, while **L'Indochine** offers gay-friendly romantic dining for those of you lucky enough to need a dinner for two.

Mon–Sat; 9am–6pm
Sun 🍴 💳
🛇 No credit cards

L'INDOCHINE
ℹ️ Beulingstraat 9
📞 627-5755
🕒 5.30pm–midnight
Tue–Sun; Closed Mon
🍴 💳 – 💳
💳 Credit cards:
AmEx, M, V

PANCAKE BAKERY
ℹ️ Prinsengracht 191
📞 625-1333
🕒 noon–9.30pm
daily 🍴 💳
💳 Credit cards:
AmEx, M, V

BARNEY'S
ℹ️ Haarlemmerstraat 102 📞 625-9761
🕒 Nov–Feb 8am–8pm daily; Mar–Oct 7am–8pm daily
🍴 💳

🛇 No credit cards

GARY'S MUFFINS
ℹ️ Marnixstraat 121
📞 638-0186
🕒 8.30am–6pm

Gary's Muffins

OUTLINES

ANNE FRANKHUIS
ℹ️ Prinsengracht 263
📞 556-7100
www.annefrank.nl
🕒 Jan–Mar, Sep–Dec 9am–7pm daily; Apr–Aug 9am–9pm daily; Closed for Yom Kippur, entrance shuts half an hour before closing time
🚋 Tram 13, 14, 17, 20
🛇 f12.50. No credit cards

Arguably the number one tourist attraction in the city, the over-whelming sea of visitors that descend upon this salute to human courage and belief is amazing when you consider how tiny the place is. Go early to avoid waiting for hours and try and shun holidays and weekends when the teaming masses of children tend to spoil

the thoughtful and serene atmosphere.

BIJBELS MUSEUM
ℹ️ Herengracht 366–8
📞 624-2436
🕒 10am–5pm Mon–Sat; 1–5pm Sun
🚋 Trams 1, 2, 5
🛇 f8. No credit cards

The good book has never given gay folk the best of raps, but if you revel in religion then the Bijbels

Museum will fascinate you. An impressive collection of bibles, as well as a basic exhibit outlining the history of Christian worship, combine to provide an exploration of all things related to this faith. As restoration is completed by summer 2002, more of the exhibit will be put on display.

HOMOMONUMENT
ⓘ Westermarkt
ⓧ All year. Special Events on Queen's Day (30 Apr), Liberation Day (4 May) and World AIDS Day (1 Dec)
ⓜ Trams 13, 14, 17
ⓒ Free

Designer Karin Daan's three pink granite triangles reach out into the Keizersgracht to celebrate the lives and losses of all who have gone before us. The world's only monument to homosexuality, the Homomonument is now a centre of gay activity on holidays, sunny afternoons and on days of great gay historical importance. Concerts and parties are often organised to celebrate the gay community, with information on events at the nearby Pink Point of Presence.

LOOIER
ⓘ Elandsgracht 109
ⓧ 11am–5pm Mon–Thu, Sat & Sun; Closed Fri
ⓜ Trams 7, 10, 17, 20
ⓒ Free

This Jordaan market specialises in antiques. Most items are no older than 150 years and the quality tends to vary from stall to stall. Digging can turn up a few finds if you're prepared to invest the time. The hushed atmosphere makes the overall experience a nice break from any hectic sightseeing schedule.

Anne Frankhuis

NOORDERMARKT

ℹ️ Noordermarkt
🕐 7.30am–1pm Mon;
Closed Tue–Sun
🚊 Trams 3, 10
💰 Free

Battling it out with the Albert Cuypmarkt for the title of best city market, the Noordermarkt is the favourite bazaar for many Amsterdammers due to its funky fashions, second-hand specials, leathers and fresh-out-of-art-school designers. This is the place to come for that secret club-wear find that you desperately need for the weekend. Not as strong a neighbour-hood focus as the Albert Cuypmarkt is for The Pijp, the Noordermarkt loses the stakes due to its one-day-only trading. Prepare for hours of sorting through the merchandise and you'll find yourself enjoying the carnival atmosphere more.

PINK POINT OF PRESENCE

ℹ️ Westermarkt
🕐 Apr–Oct noon–6pm daily
🚊 Trams 13, 14, 17
💰 Free

Make this friendly little volunteer-run joint your first stop when you arrive in Amsterdam. The wealth of gay news, pamphlets, tourist information and souvenirs on offer keeps everyone pink up to date on the latest parties and happenings going on in the city – and throughout the Netherlands. Staff at the booth would love to keeps the place open all year round, but a recent extension of their season has already stretched

Your first point of call

volunteer resources to the maximum. Try to arrive as close to noon as possible to avoid battling for information with the boyfriend of whoever is running the place on the day in question. Mobile phone use by the staff seems to rise as the day progresses.

ROMMELMARKT

ℹ️ Looiersgracht 38
🕐 11am–5pm daily
🚊 Trams 7, 10, 17, 20
💳 Free

A low-rent flea market, this place is high on sincerity and low on taste. Everything from Nana Mouskouri greatest hits collections to black velvet paintings can be picked up for a steal. But do you really want them? A nice place to see what the Dutch consider to be white trash.

THEATERMUSEUM

ℹ️ Herengracht 168
📞 551-3300
🕐 11am–5pm Tue–Fri; 1–5pm Sat; Closed Sun
🚊 Trams 13, 14, 17, 20
💳 f7.50. No credit cards

Name a famous Dutch playwright. You can't? Okay, then identify a popular Dutch play. If you're stumped, head to the Theatermuseum for a quick lesson on Dutch drama and all of its hidden gems. Don't be surprised about your complete lack of knowledge regarding any of Holland's theatrical masterpieces. Shakespeare would have been hard-pressed to come up with anything. That doesn't mean they don't try, though, and if you're a theatre fan it's worth a trip.

WESTERKERK

ℹ️ Prinsengracht 279
📞 624-7766
🕐 Tower: 10am– 5pm Mon–Sat; Closed Sun: Church: 11am–3pm Mon–Sat; Closed Sun
🚊 Trams 13, 14, 17, 20
💳 f3. No credit cards

The symbol of the Jordaan, the bells of Westerkerk no longer chime over all the district's residents, battling it out instead with the modern-day buzz of Amsterdam's increasing road traffic. The views from the bell tower remain stunning, however, owing much to the fact that Amsterdam's love of all things low marks the building out as one of the tallest structures in the city. Vertigo sufferers might want to avoid going up the shaky edifice, as strong winds can sway the tower up to 3cm. But in a neighbourhood where wandering the streets can wind you up, it makes a great landmark.

WOONBOOT-MUSEUM

ℹ️ On the canal opposite Prinsengracht 296
📞 427-0750
🕐 10am–5pm Tue–Sun; Closed Mon
🚊 Trams 13, 14, 17, 20
💳 f3.75. No credit cards

Got good sea legs? Not claustrophobic? Then take a look at what life is like aboard a real canal houseboat at the Woonbootmuseum. Surprisingly spacious inside, the museum uses prose and painting to show the past and potential of waterside living. Pick up the English guide that details some of the more confusing displays and models. This is a truly unique way of life and one that is being chosen more often by locals due to the astronomical rents and housing shortages in the city centre. It could soon become the only choice for financially challenged city dwellers.

The Old Centre: New Side

The heartbeat of the city pulses from the New Side of the Old Centre, with Centraal Station acting as the organ that pumps it. A 'carnival of souls' migrates daily to the shop-strewn streets and bright lights that line the Damrak, ending up at the chaos that the city calls Dam Square. Site of Amsterdam's first dam, the history of the square goes as far back as 1270. It was once used as a meeting point for some of Amsterdam's most controversial protests, but disgruntled youths now choose to hang out at the nearby Magna Plaza shopping centre to symbolise their dissatisfaction with society.

Tourists love this part of town with its pedestrianised alleys and modern-day shopping. It definitely makes for a nice break from the constant fear of death-by-cyclist one experiences in most of the city's other neighbourhoods.

Not so much a residential district, the New Side is home to the biggest and tattiest tourist attractions, hundreds of workaday types, internet cafés, fast-food parlours, big-time chain store shopping centres, and anything else that can make a mint from the unsuspecting masses.

A DAY OUT

For many European cities, the central railway station has often held a highly symbolic value as both a showpiece and a welcome mat to the nation. Amsterdam is no exception, as Centraal Station sits grandly at the top of the Damrak in one of the most well-located points in the city. If you're interested in railway architecture, then by all means explore the glossy interiors of the elegant structure designed by star Dutch architect PJH Cuypers. Otherwise, try and stay away at all costs, as the sea of doped-up humanity might be a little much on your sensitive pocket; the place is rife with petty thieves.

A walk down the Damrak towards Rokin exhibits Amsterdam's main contribution to the bank balances of neon manufacturers around the world. Shops specialising in nasty examples of Dutch tourist clichés line the New Side's main traffic artery, as trams whizz by from points throughout the city. Don't worry about getting to and from the area. Almost every tram in Amsterdam winds up at Centraal Station on its various journeys.

Dam Square brings the past into perspective with the Palace, Nieuwe Kerk, Nationaal Monument and Madame Tussauds all within spitting

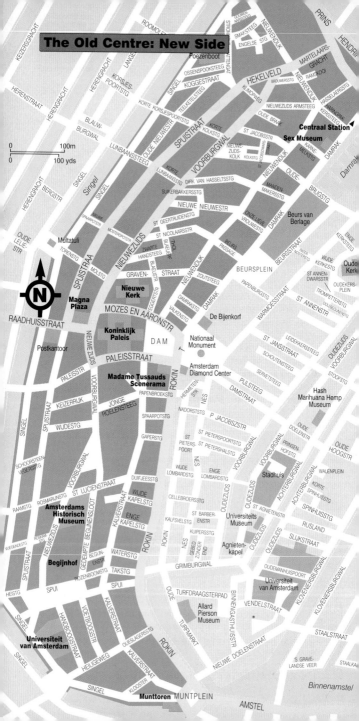

distance of each other. Spend as much time as you need to cover the sights you want and then plunge into the pedestrianised lanes of Kalverstraat and Nieuwendijk to check out the high-street fashions on offer.

But make sure to leave plenty of time to explore the highly recommended Amsterdams Historisch Museum; cut down any of the side streets that lead to Nieuwezijds Voorburgwal to prepare yourself for a wonderful afternoon learning about the religious, financial and cultural developments of the city since its founding in the 13th century. It's not as boring as it sounds.

If you're still feeling active and the weather is hot, head into the Dutch version of one-stop shopping at the Magna Plaza shopping centre. It's one of the few air-conditioned locales in the city. A massive Virgin Records store acts as a sort of meeting point for much of Amsterdam's 'so hip it hurts' youth. You might have trouble wading through the attitude at the door.

Those interested in taking a peek at the gay version of Amsterdam's Red-Light District should check out the House of Boys located on the Spui. Inside you'll find casual bars staffed by cute guys from around the world. Floor shows provide a cheaper alternative to the events that go on behind the locked doors on the upper levels.

Dam Square

Out to Lunch

FEBO

🛈 Locations through the city, with a central branch on the Damrak

🕐 24 hours daily

🍴 💰

🚫 No credit cards

Finding food that will instantly harden the arteries while simultaneously lacking any taste is a difficult task. McDonald's, Burger King and Kentucky Fried Chicken all make valiant attempts, but it's only the Dutch chain of greasy coin-operated delicacies, **Febo**, that truly manages to wrap all of these features into one micro-warmed option. You may wonder what the sullen crowds of people are doing when they pop little coins into what looks like some warped soda-pop machine. So, wonder no longer by purchasing one of Febo's oil-slick croquettes or barely-there burgers for a taste sensation I guarantee won't have you coming back for more. It's an experience every tourist has to try at least once.

OUTLINES

AMSTERDAMS HISTORISCH MUSEUM

🛈 Kalverstraat 92

📞 523-1822

www.ahm.nl

🕐 10am–5pm Mon–Fri; 11am–5pm Sat & Sun

🚋 Trams 1, 2, 4, 5, 9, 14, 16, 20, 24, 25

🎫 f12. No credit cards

Take your time to explore the buildings housing the wonderful Amsterdams Historisch Museum. They and the central courtyard are located on the original site of a 15th-century convent. The growth of the city from its 13th-century beginnings to modern-day life is mapped out in this haphazard collection of 17th-century buildings with everything from computers to Lego-like models employed to capture one's imagination. The highlight of the tour for any gay visitor comes at the end, when a mock-up of one of the city's first gay brown cafés is displayed down to the last detail. Even the dust looks original.

BEGIJNHOF

🛈 Nieuwezijds Voorburgwal 34

🕐 All year

🚋 Trams 1, 2, 4, 5, 9, 14, 16, 20, 24, 25

🎫 Free

A group of houses built around a court-yard, the Begijnhof is a secluded little gem in a neighbourhood dedicated to more on-the-go pastimes. Originally home to a group of unmarried women from well-to-do families, the Begijnhof is now the location for one of only two wooden buildings that remain in the city centre.

BEURS VAN BERLAGE

🛈 Damrak 277

📞 530-4141

🕐 10am–4pm Tue–Sun; Closed Mon

🚋 Trams 4, 9, 14, 16, 20, 24, 25

🎫 f7. No credit cards

Now a conference centre, this massive structure on the Damrak was originally built to house the city's stock exchange. Important due to its breakaway from traditional 19th-century architectural movements, the building now looks a bit out of place amidst all the tourist tat. Turn your back on the neon to imagine the place as it once was.

KONINKLIJK PALEIS

ℹ️ Dam
📞 624-8698
🌐 www.konpaleisamsterdam.nl
🕐 Jun–Aug 11am–5pm daily; Sep–May 12.30pm–5pm; days of opening vary
🚊 Trams 1, 2, 4, 5, 9, 13, 14, 16, 17, 20, 24, 25
💳 f8. No credit cards

A grand total of 13,659 wooden piles are all that separates the Koninklijk Paleis, or Royal Palace, from a watery grave. Built in the 17th century, it's no longer used as a residence for Queen Beatrice; The Hague's stately pile has since won that honour. The interiors tend to impress more than the exhaust-stained exterior, with the best external view coming from the rear. The epic size and features of the various rooms emphasise the human insignificance that average citizens were made to feel when facing the Dutch monarchs. Check tour times to ensure that the palace is not being used for any state visits.

MADAME TUSSAUDS SCENERAMA

ℹ️ Dam 20
📞 622-9239
🌐 www.madametussauds.com
🕐 10am–5.30pm daily
🚊 Trams 4, 9, 14, 16, 20, 24, 25
💳 f19.95. Credit cards: AmEx, M, V

The house of wax

SEXMUSEUM

VENUS - TEMPEL

SEX MUSEUM
AMSTERDAM

EXPOSITIE

SEX THROUGH
THE AGES

SEX DOOR DE
JAARHONDERTE

SEX DOOR DE
EEUWEN

SEX DE ETWTE
ETERNITE

Dedicated to lust

The usual wax statues of figures famous both here and abroad. Amsterdam's history and present are represented by members of the Dutch royal family and happy merchant scenes from the nation's Golden Age. Somehow slipping through the cracks were the 'lost' scenes of Catholic versus Protestant bloodshed and images of the Netherlands' greatest musical export, Boney M. Funny that.

NATIONAAL MONUMENT

🛈 Dam Square
🗓 All year
🚊 Trams 1, 2, 4, 5, 9, 13, 14, 16, 17, 20, 24, 25
💲 Free

A convenient meeting pointif you need one, this monument is dedicated to Dutch servicemen who lost their lives during World War II. Twelve urns represent the 11 provinces of the Netherlands plus their then colony of Indonesia. A facelift has been bandied about as a possibility for a number of years, but until that happens the monument remains a large phallic obelisk in the middle of a square littered with pigeon droppings.

NIEUWE KERK

🛈 Dam
📞 626-8168
www.nieuwekerk.nl
🕒 Hours vary. Call ahead to confirm times
🚊 Trams 1, 2, 4, 5, 13, 14, 16, 17, 20, 24, 25
💲 f15. No credit cards

A relative youngster on Amsterdam's church scene, the Nieuwe Kerk can 'only' trace its origins back to 1408. No longer used as a practising place of worship, the Kerk is now the venue for exhibitions, music recitals and occasions of state. Compared to the Great Fire of 1645 which gutted the area, the Reformation left few scars on the church's interior. Only a few altars and marbles were removed. A few of the city's notable poets and warmongers can be found in tombs scattered throughout the church, including PC Hoost (whose name is emblazoned on Amsterdam's designer shopping drag) and Joost van den Vondel (of Vondelpark fame, see pages 17 and 59).

SEX MUSEUM

🛈 Damrak 18
📞 622-8376
🕒 10am–11.30pm daily
🚊 Trams 4, 9, 14, 16, 20, 24, 25
💲 f5. No credit cards

Compared to Amsterdam's other museum dedicated to lust and carnality, the Erotic Museum, its close cousin the Sex Museum is a poor relation. Its location in the heart of the Damrak makes it a popular stopover for those waiting for a connection at nearby Centraal Station. But you won't miss much if you decide to keep your money in your pocket. Unlike the Erotic Museum, there are a few items of a homosexual nature, but none of it is really all that impressive.

Dam Square Monument

Window shopping

The Old Centre: Zeedijk, Red-Light District and Waterlooplein

Tracing its roots back to the earliest days of the city's formation, the Old Centre was originally home to the rich and wealthy of the city's population. Nowadays, drug dealers, prostitutes and student backpackers constitute the bulk of the neighbourhood's residents, creating a vibrant, if slightly seedy mix. Primarily known to tourists as the home of the notorious Red-Light District, the area is a maze of tiny streets, back alleys and ancient canals.

After dark is when the old centre comes into its own as the numerous neon-framed windows light up to display their wares. Girls of all shapes and sizes offer themselves up to the hordes, most with a look of utter boredom masked by their highly made-up faces.

Also home to the city's vibrant leather scene, the Warmoes-straat sees the bulk of the gay action, each bar having its own speciality. Lovers of SM, leather and rubber scenes will feel like they've died and gone to heaven.

A DAY OUT

Begin your day after a leisurely breakfast by starting at the Joods Historisch Museum and exploring the area around Waterlooplein. Here is where you'll find the sights, including the overrated Holland Experience, the Universiteit and a must-see for the art fan, Rembrandt-huis. Trams 9, 14 and 20 all cover the area, so there should be no problem finding your way there. Don't get to the neighbourhood too early as nothing opens much before 11am owing to the district's more nocturnal inclinations. Walking north from the Universiteit's main building will bring you smack-bang on to the Red-Light District's main drag, Oudezijds Achterburgwal. A number of low-rent 'museums' litter the street, including the Hash Marihuana Hemp Museum, Tattoo Museum and laughable Erotic Museum. Spend as much time as you need in each and then follow the delicate sound of church bells until you come across the welcome sight of the Oude Kerk.

Amsterdam's oldest house of worship, the Oude Kerk is a Gothic mass that rises up defiantly from the middle of the red-light action. Fans of churches should continue up the street to check out the Church in the Attic, revealed at the Museum Amstelkring. Otherwise, stop off at the Café Het Karbeel for a well-deserved cup of coffee.

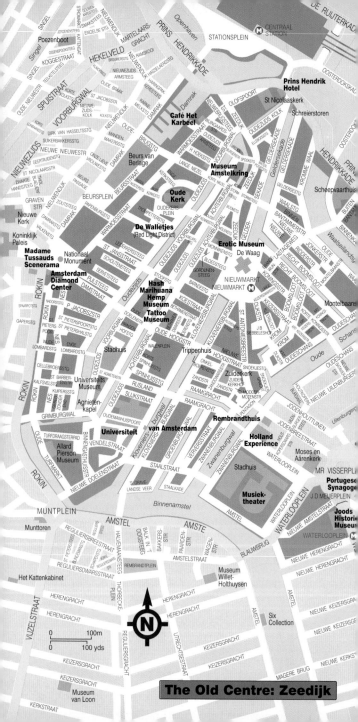

The Old Centre: Zeedijk

Straggle your way into the area called Zeedijk and you'll find yourself wandering into centuries of history. Zeedijk has always had a chequered past, often thought of as the place to get wine, women and song. Things reached a distinct low in the 1970s when you couldn't walk down the neighbourhood's streets without crunching your feet on discarded syringes. Nowadays, while the area has been cleaned up, you'll still want to keep one hand on your wallet. If you're in the mood for Chinese food, then you might want to note that Zeedijk is also home to Amsterdam's tiny Chinatown, with Nam Kee the most popular dining spot.

If you've timed it right, then you should find yourself ending up in the heart of Amsterdam's leather community, the Warmoesstraat, as the bars open. Hip hangouts, such as gay bar/restaurant Getto combine with more adventurous destinations, such as the legendary club Argos to give the Warmoesstraat its particular flavour. Places to check out during your explorations of the street include the Condomerie Het Guiden Vlies for all your condom needs, the gallery W139 for modern art with a young twist, and Cockring for hardcore clubbing nights.

 # Out to Lunch

Not known for their culinary excellence, the cafés and restaurants of the Old Centre focus their attentions on value for money. While it's not haute cuisine, a personal favourite of mine is the family-run, gay-frequented **Cafe Het Karbeel**. With people-watching and mouth-watering fondues on offer for a mere f29.50, you just can't beat it. **De Jaren**, near the Universiteit, is a swish coffee locale, with a beautiful canal-side setting that gets packed in warmer weather. Otherwise, head on over to **Nam Kee** for tasty and cheap Chinese fish

Cafe Het Karbeel

dishes. You'll have to get there pretty early, though, as the regulars tend to keep the place packed at all hours.

CAFE HET KARBEEL

- Warmoesstraat 58
- 627-4995
- 9am–1am daily
- 🍴 🍷 – 🍴
- Credit cards: AmEx, M, V

DE JAREN

- Nieuwe Doelenstraat 20-2
- 625-5771
- 10am–1am Mon–Thu & Sun; 10am–2am Fri & Sat
- No credit cards

NAM KEE

- Zeedijk 111–13
- 624-3470
- 11.30am–midnight daily
- 🍴 🍷 – 🍴
- No credit cards

OUTLINES

EROROTIC MUSEUM

| **Oudezijds**
Achterburgwal 54

| 624-7303

| 10am–5pm Mon–Sat;
1–5pm Sun

| Trams 4, 9, 14, 16, 20,
24, 25

| f10. No credit cards

Pathetic displays and haphazard cleaning create a memorable introduction to the area's sex industry, giving little in the way of history, but lots in the way of cheeky irony. Lovers of Betty Page may want to note that some of her original photographs are on display among the piles of junk. A few erotic prints doodled by Beatle John Lennon provide that little touch of respectability that this 'museum' really does try hard to avoid.

HASH MARIHUANA HEMP MUSEUM

| **Oudezijds**
Achterburgwal 148

| 623-5961

| 11am–10pm daily

| Trams 4, 9, 14, 16, 20, 24, 25

| f8. No credit cards

Seemingly created by a group of hemp-loving herbivores during a chemically-induced binge, the Hash Marihuana Hemp Museum is a celebration of all things 'high'. It doesn't hold much of interest to those who don't have a fascination with drug culture but for those curious about how a joint is rolled, it might be illuminating.

See how it's done . . .

HOLLAND EXPERIENCE

Waterlooplein 17
422-2233
www.hollandexperience.nl
10am–6pm daily
Trams 9, 14, 20
f17.50. Credit cards: AmEx, M, V

Don't waste your money at this over-priced monstrosity, catering to tourists who are more interested in sight and sound than substance. The culmination of this assault on the senses is a whizz-bang 30-minute film, edited for an MTV generation unable to focus on one image for more than a millisecond. Every Dutch cliché is pummelled at you as you examine your pockets wistfully wishing you'd kept the entrance fee safe and secure. Go instead to the Rijks-museum, Amsterdam Historisch Museum and Red-Light District to see the real thing in action. Or here's an idea – just stay on the streets and, well, experience Holland.

JOODS HISTORISCH MUSEUM

Jonas Daniel Meijerplein 2–4
626-9945
www.jhm.nl
11am–5pm daily
Trams 9, 14, 20
f10. No credit cards

Jewish history is well documented in this large building made from the remains of four synagogues in the Old Jewish Quarter. The permanent collection concentrates on the specifics of Dutch Jewish history, while the temporary exhibits provide a more global perspective. Tours of Jewish Amsterdam are offered frequently by the museum, and include visits to the nearby Portuguese Synagogue (see page 66). Phone ahead for details.

MUSEUM AMSTELKRING

Oudezijds Voorburgwal 40
624-6604
10am–5pm Mon–Sat; 1–5pm Sun
Trams 4, 9, 14, 16, 20, 24, 25
f10. No credit cards

Check out the fascinating Museum Amstelkring to see a lovingly restored and maintained piece of Amsterdam's fascinating religious history. Built in the 17th century by Roman Catholics who had been banned from worshipping the old faith, the Museum Amstelkring, or Church of the Attic, is a beautiful example of Amster-dam's religious past that still holds occasional services. Take note of the altarpiece that features paintings created by 18th-century artist Jacob de Wit. A real find.

OUDE KERK

Oudekerksplein 1
625-8284
www.oudekerk.nl
Dec–Mar 1–5pm Mon–Fri & Sun; Apr–Nov 11am–5pm Mon–Sat; 1–5pm Sun
Trams 4, 9, 16, 20, 24, 25, 26
f7.50. Exhibition charges vary. No credit cards

At night, the red neon bathes this, the oldest church in Amsterdam, in its dull glow as prostitutes bump and grind in the structure's shadow. First built in 1306, the Oude Kerk still features its original wooden roof and some fine examples of stained-glass artistry. The church comes into its own

The University

during April and May when the World Press Photo Exhibition of works by photo-journalists from all over the world comes to town.

PRINS HENDRIK HOTEL

ℹ️ Zeedijk, opposite St. Nicolaaskerk

Definitely not recommended as a place to rest your head, the Prins Hendrik is notable solely due to the fact that its front path was the last resting place of the renowned trumpeter Chet Baker. Baker plunged to his death from a window of the hotel in 1988 following a long battle with heroin. Many point to this event as the turning point in the Zeedijk's war against hard drugs, with police now claiming to have removed the most unsavoury elements from the surrounding streets. A commemorative plaque outside the hotel honours the musician for his contribution to the music world.

REMBRANDTHUIS

ℹ️ Jodenbreestraat 4
525-0400
www.rembrandthuis.nl

🕐 10am–5pm Mon–Sat; 1–5pm Sun
🚋 Trams 9, 14, 20
💳 f12.50. No credit cards

Rembrandt's original residence, the Rembrandthuis was built in 1606 and features interiors and fittings straight from the 17th century. The house is used both as an example of typical 17th-century life and as an exhibition hall for some of Rembrandt's great etchings and scribbles. Expensive for what you get, but worth the cost if you're an art admirer, and especially of course if you are an admirer of Rembrandt.

TATTOO MUSEUM

ℹ️ Oudezijds Achterburgwal 130
625-1565
www.tattoomuseum.nl
🕐 noon–5pm Tue–Sun; Closed Mon
🚋 Trams 4, 9, 16, 20, 24, 25
💳 f7.50. No credit cards

A temple to the ancient art of stabbing yourself with something sharp and injecting dye into your skin, the Tattoo Museum is actually a surprisingly enjoyable addition to the area, with a well-researched and documented collection of drawings, paintings and preserved skin slices of actual tattoos. An extensive archive and library provides a valuable resource to devotees of this ancient and painful art form.

UNIVERSITEIT VAN AMSTERDAM

ℹ️ Binnengasthuisstraat 9
525-8080
🚋 Trams 4, 9, 16, 20, 24, 25

If you have any interest in studying while in the Netherlands, then the Universiteit van Amsterdam can be a great resource. The helpline can direct you to language courses run by the Summer University, in addition to the creative courses in dance, theatre, music and visual arts offered by their arts wing, Crea. Even if you have no interest in student life, the University area is a great resource for yummy eye candy as the Dutch boys whizz their way rapidly past you in their rush to a lecture. Keep your limbs close by at all times, though, or you may lose one to a runaway bike chain.

Rijksmuseum

The Pijp and Museum Quarter

While the residents of The Pijp have no illusions of ever having the cash to buy the manors and mansions in the nearby Museum Quarter, many of its inhabitants do dream of ending up on the mansions' walls. Home to countless artists and the city's highest concentration of gay men and lesbians, The Pijp has long had a carnival-like atmosphere due in no small part to its pride and joy, the Albert Cuypmarkt. Bargains abound in this bohemian bazaar that caters to the students, immigrants and singles that call this neck-of-the-woods home.

The next couple of years should prove interesting for The Pijp as the construction of the Metro line underneath the Ferdinand Bolstraat disturbs the goings-on above ground. Residents are already bracing themselves for the onslaught of noise and traffic disturbance.

Meanwhile, the Museum Quarter continues to tick along on its pathway of elitism and exclusivity. The concentration of incredible art and designer fashions found here would be enough to sustain a small nation. Vondelpark adds to the grandeur with its offering of dappled lakes and exciting events, rounding off the neighbourhood's collection of masterpieces.

A DAY OUT

If an abandoned brewery were to be located in any town, chances are you'd find a plethora of homeless winos living inside. Amsterdam is no exception. Production closed down at the Heineken Brewery (or *Brouwerij*) amid much grumbling in 1988, and now it invites lushes the world over to explore its cavernous interiors. Considered by many to be the Dutch national drink, Heineken re-opened its doors as a tourist attraction attracting barflies from around the world to its famous all-you-can-drink beer bust that they offer at the end of their 'informative' tour.

Since 2000, Heineken has been subjecting its insides to an extensive renovation and no one really knows what is to become of the place when it re-opens, so be sure to phone ahead to check tour times. Trams 6, 7, 10, 16, 20 and 24 will take you to Heineken's front door, but it's the departure you'll need to worry about as you stumble your way to the street in a booze-filled haze.

South from Heineken on Ferdinand Bolstraat brings you to the Albert Cuypmarkt, the focal point of the neighbourhood known as The Pijp. Controversy surrounds how the area got its name, with some claiming that 'piping' (Dutch slang for giving a blow job) may have had

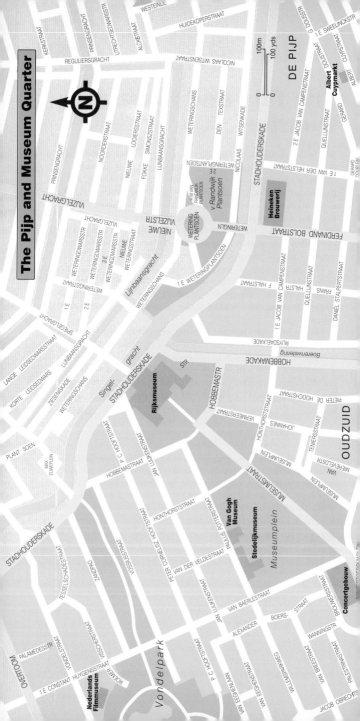

The Pijp and Museum Quarter

N

0	100m
0	100 yds

KERKSTRAAT
PRINSENGRACHT
PRINSENGRACHT
UTRECHTSEDWARSSTR
HUIDEKOPERSTRAAT
WESTEINDE

REGULIERSGRACHT
ALCOBSTRAAT
NICOLAAS WITSENSTRAAT

1 E SWEELINCKSTR
G DOUSTR

DE PIJP

NOORDERSTRAAT
LOOIERSSTRAAT
SIMONSZSTRAAT
WETERINGSCHANS
DEN TEXTSTRAAT
ALBERT
Cuypmarkt

VIJZELGRACHT
NIEUWE FOKKE
LUNBAANSGRACHT
WITSENKADE
2 E JACOB VAN CAMPENSTRAAT

VIJZELGRACHT
VIJZELGRACHT
NIEUWE WETERINGSTRAAT
NICOLAAS WETERINGPLANTSOEN
STADHOUDERSKADE
QUELLIJNSTRAAT
GERARD

NIEUWE VIJZELSTR
WIM VAN
RANDWIJK
PLANTSOEN
2 E WETERINGPLANTSOEN
1 E VAN DER HELSTSTRAAT

WETERINGDWARSSTR
3 E WETERINGDWARSSTR
WETERINGSTRAAT
v Randwijk
Plantsoen
WETERING
PLANTSOEN
WETERINGLN
FERDINAND BOLSTRAAT
Heineken
Brouwerij
GERARD

WETERINGSTRAAT
1 E
2 E
WETERINGSCHANS
Lijnbaansgracht
3 E WETERINGPLANTSOEN

SPIEGELGRACHT
LANGE LEIDSEDWARSSTRAAT
LUNBAANSGRACHT
ZIESENSKADE
WETERINGSCHANS
Singel-
gracht
STADHOUDERSKADE
1 E JACOB VAN CAMPENSTRAAT
F HALSTRAAT
HALSTR
FRANS
DANIEL STALPERTSTRAAT
QUELLIJNSTRAAT

KORTE LEIDSEDWARS
RUYSDAELKADE

PLANT SOEN
MAX
EUWERLEN
STADHOUDERSKADE
STR
Rijksmuseum
HOBBEMAKADE
Boerenwetering
HOBBEMASTR
PIETER DE HOOCHSTRAAT

STADHOUDERSKADE
HOBBEMASTRAAT
P C HOOFTSTRAAT
JAN LUIJKENSTRAAT
VERMEERSTRAAT
HONTHORSTSTRAAT
JOHANNES
TENIERSTRAAT
OUDZUID

TESSELSCHADESTRAAT
ZANDPAD
HOBBEMASTRAAT
HONTHORSTSTRAAT
PAULUS POTTERSTRAAT
Van Gogh
Museum
Stedelijkmuseum
MUSEUMSTRAAT
MUSEUMPLEIN
VAN MIEREVELDSTR
MUSEUMPLEIN

OVERTOOM
PALAMEDESSTR
1 E CONSTANT HUYGENSSTRAAT VOSSIUSSTRAAT
PETER CORNELISZ HOOFTSTRAAT
VAN DER VELDESTRAAT
Museumplein

Nederlands
Filmmuseum
ROEMER VISSCHERSTRAAT
P C HOOFTSTRAAT
VAN BAERLESTRAAT
ALEXANDER BOERS-
STRAAT
WANNINGSTR
VAN BREESTRAAT
Concertgebouw

Vondelpark
VAN EEGHENLAAN
VAN EEGHENSTRAAT
WILLEMSPARKWEG
VAN EEGHENSTRAAT
BROUWERSSTRAAT
PALESTRINASTRAAT
JACOB OBRECHTSTR

something to do with it. More likely it's the long, narrow, pipe-like streets that cemented the decision.

Ethnic foodstuffs, quirky cafés and twisted taverns give the place its character, with relatively cheap rents and apartments lending themselves to a single person's lifestyle and therefore attracting the appropriate resident crowd.

Once you've had your fill of sharp shopping in the market, turn west down Albert Cuypstraat along Ruydaelstraat till you come to the Museum Quarter's main drag, Van Baerlestraat. This major artery can be followed as long as you want, with the 'big three' museums – Van Gogh, Stedelijk and Rijksmuseum – found on the right, along the edges of the Museumplein and Vondelpark, which are further along on the left. Make sure to check out if there are any art or sporting events inside the park to fully appreciate your day. If you don't want to go inside the galleries (more fool you), you can always do the abridged version by popping into the various gift shops scattered at various points on the Museumplein's dusty lawn.

The designer shopping drag of Amsterdam is conveniently located on Peter Cornelisz Hoofstraat, with branches of Gucci, Emporio Armani, DKNY and Zegna found on the short stretch of this exclusive street. Join the in-crowd in their search for a higher purchasing plane as they root through the exclusive boutiques for their 'must haves'. After a day in the Albert Cuypmarkt, it'll certainly give you an interesting perspective on things.

Browsing around the Albert Cuypmarkt

Out to Lunch

Owing much to its ethnic roots, The Pijp is one of the best neighbourhoods in which to find a really different dish for a scrumptious supper. Surinamese food is a bit of a speciality in these parts and Amsterdam is one of the best cities in the world to try out mixed-up meals that borrow West Indian and Indonesian influences to create a cuisine it can call its own. **Albine** is a great rest-stop to try out after a long day of market shopping. If breakfast with a nouveau twist is more what your stomach has in mind, then **Bagels and Beans** should be on your list of must-eats. The outdoor patio is a great place from which to people-watch all of The Pijp's street-level life. For people-watching of a different form, then **Le Garage** should be your choice for high-end refuelling. Amsterdam's rich and somewhat famous congregate at this temple of food to see and be seen in the Hollywood atmosphere that is heightened by the millions of lightbulbs and mirrors that put one and all on display. Oh – and the grub's pretty good, too.

ALBINE
ℹ️ Albert Cuypstraat 69
📞 675-5135
🕙 10.30am–10pm Tue–Sun; Closed Mon
🍴 💳
💳 No credit cards

BAGELS AND BEANS
ℹ️ Ferdinand Bolstraat 70
📞 672-1610
🕙 8.30am–6pm Mon–Fri, 9.30am–6pm Sat, 10am–6pm Sun
🍴 💳
💳 Credit cards: AmEx, M, V

LE GARAGE
ℹ️ Beulingstraat 9
📞 627-5755
🕙 5.30pm– midnight Tue–Sun; Closed Mon
🍴 💳 – 💳
💳 Credit cards: AmEx, M, V

Lunching alfresco

OUTLINES

ALBERT CUYPMARKT

ⓘ At the junction of Albert Cuypstraat and Ferdinand Bolstraat

🕐 9.30am–5pm Mon–Sat; Closed Sun

🚋 Trams 4, 16, 24, 25

🎟 Free

Reigning queen of the 'best market in the city' contest, the Albert Cuypmarkt is the life and soul of this fun and funky neighbourhood. At the centre of the action, stalls spread out from the market's traditional location at the corner of Albert Cuypstraat and Ferdinand Bolstraat. It's definitely Amsterdam's biggest and best location for fun, food and frivolity. The general rule of thumb tends to be that the market is best for things you can put in your mouth, has great finds for things you can put on your walls' and is pretty generic when it comes to things you can put on yourself. Go for a few hours and you'll see just what I mean.

HEINEKEN BROUWERIJ

ⓘ Stadhouderskade 78

☎ 523-9239/recorded information 523-9666

A chance to sample the brew

🕐 Tours 9.30am & 11am Mon–Fri; Closed Sat & Sun

🚋 Trams 6, 7, 10, 16, 20, 24 **🎟** f2. Credit cards: AmEx, M, V

Beer, beer, glorious beer. Fill yourself right up from here to here. The Heineken Brewery is where it all started. Amsterdam's pride and joy shut down amid great protest in 1988 to reinvent itself as a huge tourist attraction. Step right up and see how beer is made! Marvel at the wonder and excitement of Heineken's marketing campaigns! Witness the wonders of fermentation! Okay, so it isn't all that exciting, but then the tour was never a reason to come here in the first place. Lushes will love the all-you-can-drink brewfest at the end of the propaganda machine. Rumours abound that the recent closure and renovations could end this Amsterdam tradition, so call ahead to confirm. Needless to say, it's the later tour that tends to fill up faster.

MUSEUMPLEIN

ⓘ Museumplein

🕐 All year **🚋** Trams 2, 3, 5, 12, 16, 20

🎟 Free

On the one hand, Museumplein is a glorious addition to the city's massive list of public green-spaces. On the other hand, it's a colossal folly outlining the lack of effectiveness of those in charge of Amsterdam's city

Van Gogh Museum 🏛
Stedelijk Museum 🏛
Concertgebouw 🎭

Making the Most of the Museums

While the museums of Amsterdam aren't on the whole expensive, true lovers of the city's massive galleries and collections might want to consider purchasing the annual Museumjaarkaart (Museum Card) for added savings. For about f55, free or reduced admission is offered at more than 400 museums and tourist traps in the city – and throughout the Netherlands. Most museums and tourist offices have the card for sale. Ask for it before you pay the full museum admission price.

If frugal is your middle name, then consider coming to the city during National Museum Week in April. Doors are flung open to collections across the country for a one-week-only art admission sale that crowds the collections to capacity.

Children-haters should not plan museum visits on weekends, during Museum Week or on Wednesday afternoons, when Dutch schoolchildren traditionally have the afternoon off. The whingeing might overwhelm you.

planning. No one misses the concrete jungle that this poky little park replaced. But, then again, the tufted grass impresses no one, nor the problematic water fountains and lighting that seem to be in a constant state of disrepair. Shame really.

NEDERLANDS FILMMUSEUM
Vondelpark 3
589-1400 www.nfm.nl
Box office: one hour before screenings; Library: 10am–5pm Tue–Fri, 11am–5pm Sat; Closed Sun–Mon Trams 1, 2, 3, 5, 6, 12, 20
f12.50. No credit cards

Dedicated to the

history of Dutch film, here art films and cinema classics are screened nightly in a jewel-like museum that occupies the grounds of a 19th-century tearoom. A library, consisting of books, magazines, photographs and

archives, makes the place a cinephile's dream. Even if film is not your thing, check out the museum to enjoy a coffee and croissant at the Cafe Vertigo inside. The view of Vondelpark from its patio is quite sublime.

Stedelijk Museum of Modern Art

AROUND TOWN

Van Gogh Museum

RIJKSMUSEUM

🛈 Stadhouderskade 42

📞 674-7047

www.rijksmuseum.nl

🕐 10am–5pm daily

🚊 Trams 2, 5, 6, 7, 10, 20

🎫 f15. Credit cards: V

The city's most popular attraction, the Rijksmuseum looms like a general overlooking its troops on the busy Stadhouderskade. You could spend all day in this palace of art, a true great in the select list of world-class art museums. If you're short on time, use the museum's handy ARIA computer system. Punch in the pieces you want to see and let the computer do the rest. It's free to use (unless you want a printout) and it'll save you precious walking time if you need to plan the quickest route to all the key treasures.

STEDELIJK MUSEUM OF MODERN ART

🛈 Paulus Potterstraat 13

📞 573-2737

www.stedelijk.nl

🕐 11am–5pm daily

🚊 Trams 2, 5, 6, 7, 10, 20

🎫 f10. No credit cards; Gift shop accepts credit cards: AmEx, M, V

Okay, so the building it's housed in is not a masterpiece, but the modern art collection of the Stedelijk is jaw-droppingly impressive for fans of 20th-century creativity. Bright, skylit rooms combine with some of the modern art world's most prized possessions to create an interior worth wandering in for a few days of delight. Big names are on display, including Andy Warhol, Stella, De Kooning, Lichtenstein, Marc Chagall and Pablo Picasso. Be warned that the museum might close briefly after recently receiving a major investment injection in order to add two sorely needed wings to its permanent exhibits. Call ahead to confirm the museum's opening status to avoid disappointment.

VAN GOGH MUSEUM

🛈 Paulus Potterstraat 7

📞 570-5200

www.vangoghmuseum.nl

🕐 10am–6pm daily

🚊 Trams 2, 3, 5, 12, 16, 20 🎫 f15.50. Credit cards: MC, V

Fans of Impressionism will not want to miss this museum dedicated to the works of Holland's most lucrative addition to the art world. A firm favourite of tourists both near and far, the gift shop is constantly packed with Japanese tourists

58 | www.outaround.com

and student types looking for that perfect Sunflower print to add to their bare white walls. Works from some of Van Gogh's contemporaries are included in the permanent exhibition in order to provide a bit of perspective to the collection. Go early to avoid getting trapped behind the busloads of travellers.

VONDELPARK

- Vondelpark
- 24 hours daily
- Trams 1, 2, 3, 5, 6, 12, 20
- Free

Town planners were having a good day when they pitched the idea of establishing a public park of lakes, pathways, forests and concert halls in the heart of Amsterdam's Museum Quarter.

Named after the controversial poet Joost van den Vondel, Vondelpark has now taken a page out of his most famous work 'Lucifer', by providing a stage for the kind of notorious living which Vondel's play was once accused of promoting. Doped-up teens, ageing hippies, speed roller-bladers and cater-wauling children descend on Vondel-park at every given opportunity, creating a kaleidoscope of activity throughout the day. Opened in 1865, Vondelpark now features park-sponsored arts events, rock concerts, film screenings and a summer-long festival of open-air theatre. Sporty types should join the Friday Night Skate for local roller-bladers, while non-sporty types should stay away to prevent themselves from grave physical harm.

A quiet corner of Vondelpark

A Hortus Botanicus hothouse

The Plantage and the Oost

It's time to get your comfiest clogs on, as this combination of neighbourhoods is sure to tucker you out. A collection of high-class residences with earthy garden havens, the sights of the Plantage and the Oost cater to a variety of tastes. Often overlooked as a tourist destination due to its distance from the centre of the city, the area holds a wealth of diamond-in-the-rough museums and architectural delights that should not be missed.

Jewish history and tradition abound in the Plantage, revolving heavily around the Portuguese Synagogue. Festivals and events in the area often reflect the multiculturalism of the region, celebrating the ethnic mix and cultural values of this vibrant melange of immigrants and yuppies.

If you need a rest during your travels, the Oost is the best place to go, with a number of lush parks and picturesque gardens available for a brief retreat.

A DAY OUT

The day begins early with a trek out to the Tropenmuseum, an intriguing collection of interactive exhibits and re-creations designed to highlight what life is like in the tropics. The Tropenmuseum is the furthest point out of the city you will probably venture to, but it's worth the extra time required. Trams 9, 10 or 14 will drop you at its doorstep. If you want to make the commitment, go a little further out and you'll be able to spot the only real windmill within easy travel distance from downtown. It's been converted into a brewery, but its appeal lies in the sheer Dutch kitsch value.

Proceed down Plantage Middelaan towards Amsterdam's hub, and you'll discover the heavily advertised Artis Zoo, the calmly beautiful Hortus Botanicus (Botanical Gardens), and slightly off the main street, the Verzetsmuseum (Museum of the Dutch Resistance). The Hortus is a nice jaunt simply because of the stunning variety of tropical plants on view in the many greenhouses. The Dutch East India Company started the ball rolling back in 1632 when it brought tropical seeds and plants back from its various ports of call. Some of those specimens still grow in the gardens today.

If Jewish history is one of your priorities then continue down towards the site of the final assembly point that Jewish people faced before deportation, the Hollandse Schouwburg. The Plantage was originally the centre of the Jewish diamond trade and was transformed by diamond

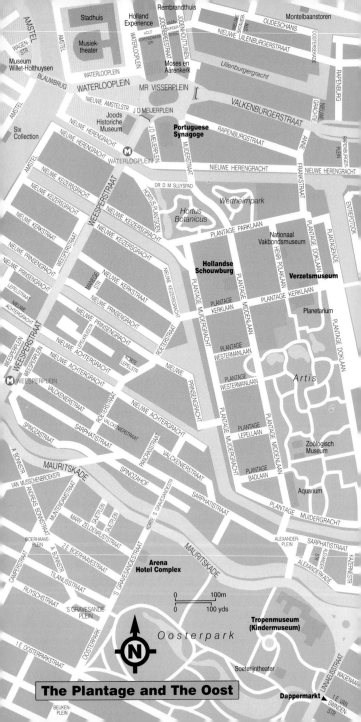

money during the 19th century. World War II left its mark indelibly on the area, as the once thriving Jewish community is now a shell of its former self. The Portuguese Synagogue on the border with the Old Centre makes a great end to an epic day, capturing the essence of the neighbourhood's formerly ultra-kosher flavour.

If you're not in a rush, kick your day off a little earlier by exploring the working-class neighbourhoods found just beyond the site of the Tropenmuseum. Check out what's going on in the Dappermarkt, a very down-to-earth shopping experience that relies more on everyday household goods than clothing bargains for the bulk of its trade. It's not exactly Chanel, but it's a nice slice of what real Amsterdam looks like.

 # Out to Lunch

Owing to the workaday roots of the residents of the Oost, bars, cafés and restaurants tend to leave a lot to be desired. Recent influxes of yuppies have begun to change matters, with rest stops like the stylish cappuccino corners of **East of Eden** and African cuisine specialist **Kilimanjaro** offering greater options. For a truly Dutch experience, stop off at **Brouwerij t'IJ**, a swanky little brewery located in the heart of a windmill. Otherwise, pick up some nibbles at the **Sterk** deli in Waterlooplein (which is technically in the Old Centre) for yummies you can have on the go.

BROUWERIJ T'IJ

🛈 Funenkade 7
📞 622-8325
🕗 3–8pm Wed–Sun; Closed Mon & Tue
🍴 Bar only. No food.
💳 No credit cards

EAST OF EDEN

🛈 Linnaeusstraat 11
📞 665-0743
🕗 11am–1am Mon–Thu; 11am–3am Fri & Sat
🍴 Light meals only.
💳 No credit cards

KILIMANJARO

🛈 Rapenburger-plein 6
📞 622-3485
🕗 5–10pm Tue–Sun; Closed Mon
🍴 🏷
💳 Credit cards: AmEx. M, V

STERK

🛈 Waterlooplein 241
📞 626-5097
🕗 8am–2am daily
💳 Credit cards: M, V

Watch the world go by as you lunch

OUTLINES

ARENA HOTEL COMPLEX

🛈 's Gravesandestraat 51

📞 694-7444

www.hotelarena.nl

🚋 Trams 3, 6, 9, 10, 14

💳 Credit cards: AmEx, M, V

This one's for the architecture buffs. The Arena Hotel is a sprawling bar/hotel/club/restaurant complex that tends to draw many a local to its swish interiors. While it's not a gay hotspot and it's a little too out-of-the-way to warrant approval as a recommended place to rest your head, the Arena might be just what you need if you're interested in seeing how the buildings of yesterday are being transformed into the masterpieces of tomorrow.

ARTIS ZOO

🛈 Plantage Kerklaan 38–40

📞 523-3400

🕐 9am–5pm daily

🚋 Trams 6, 9, 14, 20

💳 f28.50. No credit cards

Lions and tigers and bears, oh my! Like most other urban European zoos, the Artis Zoo is short on space, doing the best

Artis Zoo – the place for bears

they can with the acreage they've been given. Indoor 'rainforest' simulations and mock terrains give insight into international animal habitats, but then you've probably seen this all before. If you want to check out what lives in the Amsterdam canals, take a look at the aquariums. Be sure to have taken that romantic canal ride *before* doing this, however, or you probably won't want to go anywhere near the water. A planetarium and natural science museum make up the rest of the zoo's offerings. A word of caution: if you don't like children, avoid this place at all costs.

DAPPERMARKT

🛈 Dapperstraat

🕐 9am–5pm Mon–Sat; Closed Sun

🚋 Trams 3, 6, 10, 14

💳 No credit cards

A nice way to discover 'real' Amsterdam, Dappermarkt has all the usual stuff along with cheap clothes and underwear (although not much you'd want to fight for). Think Calvin Clone. Prices are cheap and you never know what you'll find if you have a good hunt around for it. As per usual, credit cards at this market are a no go.

HOLLANDSE SCHOUWBURG

🛈 Plantage Middenlaan 24

📞 626-9945

🕐 11am–4pm daily

🚊 Trams 7, 9, 14, 20

🎟 Free

Originally a theatre, the Hollandse Schouwburg was the last stop in Amsterdam for thousands of Jews rounded up through-out the city before their deportation to Nazi Germany's concentration camps. Between 60,000 and 80,000 Jews passed their way through the theatre's doors, most joining the list of 104,000 Dutch Jews who never returned to their homes in the Netherlands. While most of the original theatre fittings have been removed, an exhibition has been installed to help illuminate the plight of the country's valiant Jewish community.

HORTUS BOTANICUS

ℹ️ Plantage Middenlaan 2A

☎ 625-8411

🕐 Apr–Oct 9am–5pm Mon–Fri; 11am–5pm Sat–Sun. Nov–Mar 9am–4pm Mon–Fri; 11am–4pm Sat–Sun

🚊 Trams 7, 9, 14, 20

🎟 Apr–Oct f10. Nov–Mar f7.50. No credit cards

Founded in 1632 by the Dutch East India Company, the Hortus Botanicus has grown considerably since a few tropical seeds were planted almost four centuries ago. Some of the original specimens still grow in the various hothouses and structures built to show off the Botanical Gardens' impressive collection. Desert, tropical and sub-tropical conditions are maintained in various greenhouses scattered throughout the grounds, while a pleasant terrace gives

Gateway to the tropical gardens

you a chance to rest and relax in the junglish surroundings.

KINDERMUSEUM

- Linnaeusstraat 2
- 568-8300
- www.tropenmuseum.nl
- 10am–5pm Mon–Fri; noon–5pm Sat–Sun
- Trams 9, 10, 14
- f12.50. No credit cards

Technically an addition to the Tropenmuseum, the Kindermuseum is an all-Dutch museum geared towards children. If you're a child at heart and you're already at the Tropenmuseum, then

you might as well enjoy the fun. None of the exhibits have English translations, but you'll enjoy the selection of foreign films on offer in the cinema.

OOSTERPARK

- Oosterpark
- Trams 3, 6, 9, 14

The green space of the East, Oosterpark is the district's crown jewel. The park explodes with action in May when the first week of the month brings the Oosterparkfestival, a celebration of

multiculturalism and international understanding.

PORTUGUESE SYNAGOGUE

- Mr Visserplein 3
- 624-5351
- www.esnoga.com
- Apr–Oct 10am–4pm Mon–Fri, Sun; Closed Sat; Nov–Mar 10am–4pm Mon–Thu; 10am–3pm Fri; Closed Sat & Sun
- Trams 4, 9, 14, 20
- f7.50. No credit cards

The heart of Amsterdam's once thriving Jewish community, the Portuguese Synagogue is the oldest and largest synagogue in

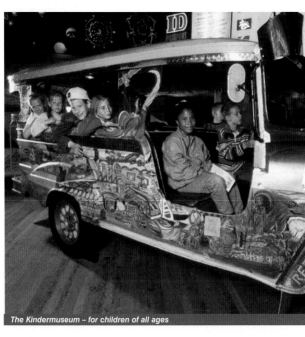

The Kindermuseum – for children of all ages

Exotic exhibits on display at the Tropenmuseum

the city. Still in use as a place of worship.

TROPENMUSEUM

- ℹ️ Linnaeusstraat 2
- ☎️ 568-8215
- www.tropenmuseum.nl
- 🕙 10am–5pm Mon–Fri; noon–5pm Sat & Sun
- 🚊 Trams 9, 10, 14
- 🎟️ f12.50. No credit cards

A real must-see and worth the trek, the Tropenmuseum is probably the only museum in the world dedicated to life in the tropics and the effects of European colonialism. It's hard to believe that the museum originally began life as a celebration of all things good about Dutch colonial practices. Looking now at the shattered economies and corrupt governments of Indonesia and Surinam, you can't help but wonder what they were thinking. Artefacts and everyday goods illuminate the trials and tribulations of past lives. Don't miss this.

VERZETSMUSEUM

- ℹ️ Plantage Kerklaan 61
- ☎️ 620-2535
- 🕙 10am–5pm Tue–Fri; noon–5pm Sat & Sun
- 🚊 Trams 6, 9, 14, 20
- 🎟️ f8. No credit cards

Interested in World War II memorabilia? Then come on down to this showroom documenting the Dutch Resistance efforts during the bleak war years. Spy gadgets, trick doors, underground papers and secret espionage techniques are all discussed in detail. Avoid the silly film at the end of the exhibit and you'll leave the museum feeling much better about the gallery's contents.

Not just a girl's best friend?

All Shopped Out

It's a sad fact to face, but shopping is not one of the highlights of a trip to Amsterdam. Paris offers better deals and a wider selection of designer merchandise, while London is better known for its funky street style. Trend-conscious Dutch shoppers tend to be followers rather than leaders. Second-hand wear and cutting-edge furniture are better buys, with fabulous finds available if you dig.

And wherever you go, you can count on the service being dire. Don't worry if you're just browsing. The chances of being approached by anyone resembling a helpful employee rank as high as finding the proverbial snowball in hell.

Top of the Shops

Amsterdam Diamond Centre

ℹ️ Rokin 1–5 *See map p. 44.*
📞 624-5787
🕐 10am–6pm Mon–Wed, Fri–Sun; 10.30am–8:30pm Thu
🚋 Trams 4, 9, 14, 16, 20, 24, 25
💳 Credit cards: AmEx, DC, M, V

Diamonds are forever and the Amsterdam Diamond Centre does its utmost to convince you that eternity should be bought from them. Tours of their facilities can be arranged at a moment's notice, but the pressure to buy can be intense.

Club Wear House

ℹ️ Herengracht 265 *Herengracht: map p. 28.*
📞 622-8766 www.clubwearhouse.nl
🕐 noon–6pm Tue & Wed, Fri & Sat; noon–8pm Thu; closed Sun & Mon
🚋 Trams 1, 2, 5, 13, 17, 20 💳 Credit cards: AmEx, DC, M, V

ALL SHOPPED OUT

Club kids flock to this tiny temple of style where trends and T-shirts whizz out the door faster than you can say 'speed garage'. Friendly staff, all knowledgeable about the latest fashions, current stock and the party scene of the city, distribute club flyers and advice to anyone who's interested.

Frozen Fountain

ℹ Prinsengracht 629 *Prinsengracht: map p. 20* 📞 622-9375 ⏰ 1–6pm Mon, 10am– 6pm Tue–Fri, 10am–5pm Sat; Closed Sun 🚊 Trams 1, 2, 5 💳 No credit cards

A mix of home furnishings, fashion accessories and basic coolness, Frozen Fountain has a high hip rating that will make you want to purchase everything in sight. Don't be dissuaded by the holier-than-thou staff; the Dutch design is worth the hassle.

Housewives on Fire

ℹ Spuistraat 102 *Spuistraat: map p. 36* 📞 422-1067 www.xs4all.nl/~housew ⏰ 10am–7pm Mon–Wed, Fri & Sat; 10am–9pm Thu; Closed Sun (except May–Aug noon–6pm Sun) 🚊 Trams 1, 2, 5 💳 Credit cards: M, V

A hair salon, live DJ, outrageous accessories and a wild collection of new and abused clothing make Housewives on Fire the best place in the city to pick up some flashy fashions. Refreshing for its friendliness, it is also the place to collect flyers and tickets to upcoming club-scene events and parties. A can't-miss cultivator of Amsterdam's club-kid crowd.

Intermale

ℹ Spuistraat 251 *Spuistraat: map p. 36* 📞 625-0009 www.intermale.nl ⏰ 10am–6pm Mon–Wed, Fri & Sat, 10am–9pm Thu; Closed Sun 🚊 Trams 1, 2, 4, 5, 9, 14, 16, 20, 24, 25 💳 Credit cards: M, V

Intermale

Described as Europe's largest gay bookshop, Intermale carries an extensive number of books and magazines, crossing the entire spectrum of gay literature.

Great gay fiction can be found spread along the display shelves on the left of the store, while pornography is located on the right and in the main entrance.

Kitsch Kitchen

ℹ️ Rozengracht 183 *Rozengracht: map p. 20* 📞 622-8261 🕐 10am–6pm Mon–Sat; Closed Sun 🚊 Trams 13, 14, 17, 20 💳 Credit cards: AmEx, DC, M, V

You'll need a pair of sunglasses when shopping inside this boutique. Specialising in all things bright and beautiful, Kitsch Kitchen imports anything and everything designed to make your home a little more garish and a lot more fun.

Metz & Co.

ℹ️ Leidsestraat 34–6 *See map p. 20* 📞 520-7030 🕐 9:30am–6pm Mon–Wed, Fri & Sat,9:30am–9pm Thu, noon–5pm Sun 🚊 Trams 1, 2, 5, 20 💳 Credit cards: AmEx, DC, M, V

Quality comes at a price, and boy does this exclusive department store know it. The well-appointed men's department on the third floor offers a range of designer gear, including Alexander McQueen, Hugo Boss and Iceberg – all with price tags to match. Sale periods in January and June can bring a few bargains to light. Just don't go looking for anything too outrageous.

One of the city's numerous gay bookshops

ALL SHOPPED OUT

Mexican glitter

Santa Jet

ℹ️ Prinsenstraat 7
Prinsenstraat: map p. 28
📞 427-2070
🕐 11am–6pm Mon–Fri, 10am–5pm Sat, noon–5pm Sun 🚊 Trams 1, 2, 5, 20
💳 Credit cards: AmEx, DC, M, V

Mexican artwork, mirrors and house-wares collide in the explosive mass of colour that is Santa Jet. Specialising in collectors' works by Mexican artists, everything from Day of the Dead candlesticks to mobile Christ altars are available at very affordable prices. It'll be enough to make you want to scream 'Olé!'.

RoB

Leather goods

ℹ️ Weteringschans 253
Weteringschans p. 20
📞 625-4686
www.rob.nl 🕐 11am–7pm Mon–Wed, 11am–8pm Thu, 11am–6pm Sat; Closed Sun 🚊 Trams 6, 7, 10 💳 Credit cards: AmEx, M. V

If you're serious about your leather and want the very best, then the world's most famous outfitter for fans of cowhide should not be missed. In existence for more than 25 years, RoB caters to the leatherman who knows what he wants and how he wants it. Their famous 501 model jeans will set you back about 346 euros, but the quality speaks for itself. Waiting lists for tailored gear can be as long as ten weeks, so plan in advance if you want custom clothing.

A second branch, specialising in accessories, can be found at Warmoesstraat 32.

Sissy Boy

ℹ️ Kalverstraat 199
Kalverstraat: map p. 44
📞 638-9305
www.sissy-boy.nl
🕐 noon–6pm Sun, Mon; 10am–6pm Tue, Wed, Fri & Sat; 10am–9pm Thu
🚊 Trams 1, 2, 4, 5, 9, 14, 16, 20, 24, 25
💳 Credit cards: AmEx, DC, M, V

High-street shopping with a distinctly Dutch twist. Big names like French Connection share the racks with own label 'Made in Holland' Sissy Boy products for an overall look of good basics and wardrobe additions at prices that won't make you gag.

BOOKSHOPS

ATHENAEUM NIEUWSCENTRUM

🛈 Spui 14–16
📞 622-6248
www.athenaeum.nl
🕑 10am–8pm Mon–Wed Fri & Sat; 10am–10pm Thu; 11am–7pm Sun
🚊 Trams 1, 2, 5
💳 Credit cards: AmEx, DC, M, V

Newspapers, periodicals, magazines and journals from around the globe are stocked here, a favourite amongst Amsterdam's intellectuals. If they don't have it, they'll do their utmost to get it for you.

VROLIJK

🛈 Paleisstraat 135
📞 623-5142
www.xs4all.nl/~vrolijk
🕑 11am–6pm Mon–Wed & Fri; 11am–9pm Thu; 11am–5pm Sat; Closed Sun
🚊 Trams 1, 2, 5
💳 Credit cards: AmEx, DC, M, V

Amsterdam's other gay bookstore, Vrolijk specialises in Dutch publications, leaving the English stuff to Intermale (featured on page 70). Less floorspace is dedicated to porn than Intermale, but there is also less

literature and more gay 'giftware'.

WATERSTONE'S

🛈 Kalverstraat 152
📞 638-3821
www.waterstones.co.uk
🕑 11am–6pm Sun & Mon; 9am–6pm Tue & Wed; 9am–9pm Thu; 9am–7pm Fri; 10am–7pm Sat
🚊 Trams 1, 2, 4, 5, 9, 14, 16, 20, 24, 25
💳 Credit cards: AmEx, M, V

A branch of the well-respected British bookstore chain, Waterstone's carries the largest selection of books in English found in Amsterdam.

CLUBWEAR

CYBERDOG

🛈 Spuistraat 250
📞 330-6385
www.clubwearhouse.nl
🕑 noon–6pm Tue & Wed, Fri & Sat; noon–8pm Thu; Closed Sun & Mon
🚊 Trams 1, 2, 5, 13, 17, 20
💳 Credit cards: AmEx, DC, M, V

If you want something to wear that'll glow in the dark, pulse to the beat of the music, is 3-D or has a bit of neon attached to it, then you'll find it here.

DEPARTMENT STORES

DE BIJENKORF
ℹ De Bijenkorf Dam 1
☎ 621-8080
www.bijenkorf.nl
🕐 11am–6pm Mon;
9:30am–6pm Tue & Wed,
Fri & Sat; 9:30am–9pm Thu,
noon–6pm Sun
🚋 Trams 1, 2, 4, 5, 9, 13,
14, 16, 17, 20, 24, 25
💳 Credit cards: AmEx,
DC, M, V

Striving to be the Harrod's of Amsterdam, De Bijenkorf misses wildly. While the selection of goods is quite strong, the fashions on offer fail to impress. The window displays at Christmas are stunning, but it does feel a bit like the technicians go on holiday for the other 364 days of the year, judging by the snore-inducing mannequin scenes.

DESIGNER GOODS

DKNY
ℹ PC Hoofstraat 60
☎ 671-0554
🕐 noon–6pm Mon;
10am–6pm Tue, Wed & Fri;
10am–9pm Thu; noon–6pm
Sat
🚋 Trams 3, 12
💳 Credit cards: AmEx,
DC, M, V

A largish branch of the popular American designer store (the name stands for Donna Karan New York), with goodies for men, women and children.

ERMENEGILDO ZEGNA
ℹ PC Hoofstraat 70
☎ 670-4477
🕐 9.30am–6pm Mon–
Wed, Fri & Sat; 9.30am–
9pm Thu, noon–5pm Sun
🚋 Trams 3, 12
💳 Credit cards: AmEx,
DC, M, V

Take it home . . .

Conservative, yet well-constructed Italian shoes, shirts, suits and ties.

GUCCI

🛈 PC Hoofstraat 58
⌚ 1–6pm Mon; 10am–6pm Tue–Wed & Fri; 10am–9pm Thu, 10am–5.30pm Sat
🚋 Trams 3, 12
💳 Credit cards: AmEx, DC, M, V

Fans of the house that Gucci built need not panic; a small branch of the famed leather and clothing designer is located in Amsterdam, with a limited selection of goods.

KENNETH COLE

🛈 Leidsestraat 20-22
⌚ 627-6012
www.kencole.com
⌚ noon–6pm Mon–Wed, Fri & Sat; 10am–9pm Thu; 1–5pm Sun
🚋 Trams 1, 2, 5
💳 Credit cards: AmEx, DC, M, V

A wide selection of conservative own-brand shoes, leathers and jackets.

Cuts and Curls

MULBERRY

🛈 PC Hoofstraat 46
⌚ 673-8086
⌚ 1–6pm Mon; 10am–6pm Tue–Sat; Closed Sun
🚋 Trams 3, 12
💳 Credit cards: AmEx, DC, M, V

Designer leathers and cases from the classic streets of Olde England.

HEALTH AND BEAUTY

CONDOMERIE HET GUIDEN VLIES

🛈 Warmoesstraat 141
⌚ 627-4174
www.condomerie.com
⌚ 11am–6pm Mon–Sat; Closed Sun
🚋 Trams 4, 9, 14, 16, 20, 24, 25
💳 Credit cards: AmEx, DC, M, V

Novelty condoms and a mini-museum make this boutique the largest in Europe dedicated to our pal the prophylactic.

CUTS AND CURLS

🛈 Korte Leidsedwars-straat 74
⌚ 624-6881
⌚ 10am–8pm Mon–Sat; Closed Sun
🚋 Trams 6, 7, 10
💳 No credit cards

Haircuts and colours for the leatherman

and his friends. Styles cost f44.

HIGH STREET

MEXX

🛈 Kalverstraat 178
⌚ 11am–6pm Mon; 9.30am–6pm Tue & Wed, Fri & Sat; 9.30am–9pm Thu; noon–6pm Sun
🚋 Trams 1, 2, 4, 5, 9, 14, 16, 20, 24, 25
💳 Credit cards: AmEx, DC, M, V

The Dutch version of high-street shopping, Mexx is sort of like a classy Gap. Basic black tends to be the colour of choice most seasons, making it a good place to buy quality separates.

LEATHER, RUBBER AND LATEX

BLACK BODY

🛈 Lijnbaansgracht 292
⌚ 626-2553
www.blackbody.nl
⌚ 10am–6.30pm Mon–Fri; 11am–6pm Sat; Closed Sun
🚋 Trams 6, 7, 10
💳 Credit cards: M, V

Specialists in rubber and latex gear, Black Body is continental Europe's best location for those in need of waders, masks, toys

Holland

The traditional souvenir

and clothing. Staff are extremely helpful and are willing to assist both first-timers and experienced fetishists with their purchases.

MISTER B

ⓘ Warmoesstraat 89
✆ 422-0003
www.mrb.nl
🕐 10am–6.30pm Mon–Fri; 11am–6pm Sat; 1–6pm Sun
🚊 Trams 4, 9, 14, 16, 20, 24, 25
💳 Credit cards: M, V

Mister B covers all the bases of rubber and leather wear. Its location on Warmoesstraat makes it a great place to browse while you prepare for an evening's entertainment. Tattoos and piercings are also on offer.

MUSIC

VIRGIN MEGASTORE

ⓘ Magna Plaza, Nieuwezijds Voorburgwal 182
✆ 622-8929
🕐 11am–7pm Mon; 10am–7pm Tue & Wed, Fri & Sat; 10am–9pm Thu, noon–7pm Sun
🚊 Trams 1, 2, 5, 13, 17, 20
💳 Credit cards: AmEx, DC, M, V

CDs, DVDs, accessories and everything else you expect from the huge multi-national.

SEX SHOPS

BRONX

ⓘ Kerkstraat 53–55
✆ 623-1548
🕐 noon–midnight daily
🚊 Trams 1, 2, 5, 11
💳 Credit cards: M, V

A large selection of videos, DVDs and a limited number of magazines with a slight slant towards bear and leatherman porn.

DRAKE'S

ⓘ Damrak 61
✆ 627-9544
🕐 9am–1am Sun–Thu; 9am–2am Fri & Sat
🚊 Trams 1, 2, 4, 5, 9, 13, 14, 16, 17, 20, 24, 25
💳 Credit cards: M, V

Much like Bronx, the cinema attached to the main shop is often busy after work and during lunch hours.

SOUVENIRS

WOODEN SHOE FACTORY

ⓘ Nieuwe Hoogstraat 11
✆ 427-3862
www.woodenshoefactory.nl
🕐 9am–6pm daily

Bronx

🚊 Trams 1, 2, 5
💳 Credit cards: AmEx, DC, M, V

If you fancy yourself in a pair of clogs, then the Wooden Shoe Factory should be a must on your list. All shapes and sizes are available. Just don't wear the things around town or you'll be branded a stupid tourist.

VINTAGE AND SECONDHAND

WINI

ⓘ Haarlemmerstraat 29
✆ 427-9393
🕐 1–6pm Mon; 10am–6pm Tue & Wed, Fri & Sat; 10am–9pm Thu; Closed Sun
🚊 Trams 1, 2, 4, 5, 9, 13, 14, 16, 17, 20, 24, 25
💳 No credit cards

While the men's collection is small, the pieces on offer are just sizzling. Retro fashions and plush polyesters make Wini a good place for 1970s-styled threads.

Gary Christmas and friend

Eating Out

Amsterdam isn't really known as a culinary capital, but its reputation is improving with the addition of a few hip hang-outs. Restaurants considered the best in town aren't necessarily so because of the quality of the food. Currently leading the pack with the in-crowd are Inez IPSC, the Supper Club and Le Garage. Dutch cuisine relies heavily on local cheeses and the ever-present pancake. Do make sure to try Indonesian and Surinamese food while you're in town; one of the few welcome outcomes of Holland's colonial past.

Cream of the Cuisine

Backstage

Utrechtsedwarsstraat 67 | 622-3638 | 10am–5.30pm Mon–Sat; Closed Sun | Trams 4, 6, 7, 10 | | | No credit cards

The Backstage is not so much a café as an experience. Twins Greg and Gary Christmas started it over 30 years ago after a life in showbiz that took them all over the world. A typical day sees ballet dancers and Church of Satan priests congregating to bask in the glow of both the radiant sweaters on offer and the charisma of the surviving twin, Gary. If you're lucky, he will serve you up a dose of fortune-telling in addition to any of the wittily named sandwiches on the menu. Plan to stay for an hour, yet spend the whole day. You'll be glad you did.

The following price guides have been used for eating out and indicate the price for a main course :

= cheap = under f15

= moderate = f15–30

= expensive = over f30

De Jaren

🛈 Nieuwe Doelenstraat 20–2

☎ 625-5771 🕒 10am–1am Mon–Thu
& Sun; 10am–2am Fri–Sat

🚊 Trams 4, 9, 14, 16, 20, 24, 25

🍴 🍷 – 🍽 💳 No credit cards

The advantages of going to the
gym every day become clear
when you decide to embark on a
jaunt to the grand café De Jaren.
The outdoor patio, overlooking
one of the more picturesque
points of the Amstel, is a crowded,
seething mass on sunny days and
your muscles will come in handy
when attempting to shove
someone from their prized
canalside table. Inside, the vaulted
interior makes for a pleasant place
to spend a few hours sipping a
coffee or catching up on
international news from any of the
numerous periodicals available for
perusal. Try and go on a weekday
to fully appreciate the light and
space of the place.

Le Garage

🛈 Beulingstraat 9

☎ 627-5755

🕒 5.30pm–midnight Tue–Sun; Closed Mon

🚊 Trams 3, 5, 6, 12, 16, 20

🍴 🍷 – 🍽 💳 Credit cards: AmEx, DC, M, V

Celebrity gay chef Joop Braakhekke
runs Le Garage like a well-oiled
machine. Air kisses and facelifts flood
the spotlit stage – I mean restaurant –
as waiters whisk dish after dish onto the tables of Amsterdam's rich and
famous. French cuisine provides the backbone of the menu, with
occasional nods to foreign influences. The drama on the plate is
gripping, even if the action going on around you sometimes overtakes it.
Is the food worth it? Yes.

Try it for yourself – at Backstage

Downtown

🛈 Reguliersdwars-straat 31

☎ 622-9958

🕒 10am–7pm daily

🚊 Trams 1, 2, 4, 5, 9, 14, 16, 20,
24, 25 🍴 🍷

💳 No credit cards

Gay boys in need of a quick
bite head on over to
Downtown to fill their
well-toned tums.

While the service isn't the
greatest, the outdoor patio
makes up for it on sunny days
and weekends. On weekend
mornings this is a great place
to see who picked up whom
the night before as the various
couples inevitably end up
here nursing their pounding
hangovers. Prices are
reasonable, but it's the people-
watching that really warrants
the cost.

Tasty snacks at Gary's Muffins

Gary's Muffins

ℹ️ Marnixstraat 121
📞 638-0186
🕐 8.30am–6pm
Mon–Sat; 9am–6pm Sun
🚊 Trams 10, 17
🍴 🍷 –
💳 No credit cards

A popular breakfast spot, Gary's Muffins serves up a variety of wholesome, organic bagels and muffins to the hungry masses. A favourite amongst local white-collar types, Gary's also has a phone-in delivery service for those on the go. Check out the community noticeboards for info on local happenings and events. A branch on the Reguliersdwarsstraat is a gay hotspot for late-night snacks.

Getto

ℹ️ Warmoesstraat 51
📞 421-5151
🕐 5pm–1am Tue–Sun;
Closed Mon
🚊 Trams 4, 9, 16, 20, 24, 25 🍴 🍷 – 🍷
💳 Credit cards: DC, M, V

It's a bar. No, it's a restaurant. Getto is actually anything it damn well wants to be. A gay favourite, it offers a variety of delicious meals, with a

A gay favourite

number of veggie options. Strangely located in the heart of the Warmoesstraat, you can't help thinking that the proprietor should really have opened the place on the Reguliersdwarsstraat.

The exciting result is a mix of a Red-Light District boozer with the model-like clientele more often found in other gay neighbourhoods. Bingo is run every Thursday night, while the Happy Hour of 5-7pm draws a funky crowd.

The second Monday of every month sees the place open up for women only.

Hemelse Modder

- ℹ️ Oude Waal 9
- 📞 624-3203
- 🕐 6pm–midnight Tue–Sun; Closed Mon
- 🚊 Trams 1, 2, 4, 5, 9, 13, 16, 17, 20, 24, 25
- 💳 Credit cards: AmEx, DC, M, V

Mediterranean food in an intimate setting, this place is perfect for a romantic dinner with someone you love.

Friendly staff and a candlelit vibe add to the cosy ambience. The place is gay owned and operated, but attracts a mixed crowd who are drawn by the restaurant's combination of subtle yet efficient service and irresistible edibles. Vegetarian options are available.

Inez IPSC

- ℹ️ Amstel 2
- 📞 639-2899
- 🕐 noon–3pm, 7–11.30pm daily
- 🚊 Trams 4, 9, 20
- 💳 Credit cards: M, V

Considered by those in the know to be the hottest restaurant in town, weekend reservations can be tricky if you don't have connections. The view of the city is stunning, and when combined with the interiors designed by Peter Giele (once the artistic mind behind the late gay nightclub legend, the Roxy), the experience can be overwhelming. The presentation of the sublime international cuisine matches its surroundings. It's worth the investment.

Pancake Bakery

- ℹ️ Prinsengracht 191
- 📞 625-1333
- 🕐 noon–9.30pm daily
- 🚊 Trams 13, 17, 20
- 💳 Credit cards: AmEx, DC, M, V

Sweet and savoury pancakes constitute the bulk of the menu options at this tiny basement dining spot with a very Olde Dutch feel. Everything from the traditional lemon and sugar crêpe to speciality pancakes filled with peaches, cherry liquor and ice-cream are on offer.

The Supper Club

- ℹ️ At the Junction of Albert Cuypstraat and Ferdinand Bolstraat, Jonge Roelensteeg 21
- 📞 638-0513
- 🌐 www.supperclub.nl
- 🕐 8pm–1am daily
- 🚊 Trams 1, 2, 5, 13, 17
- 🍽️ Set menu
- 💳 Credit cards: AmEx, DC, M, V

For my money, the Supper Club is the hippest place in town. Beds replace chairs as diners lounge on comfy mattresses to eat their tasty treats in sleepy splendour. Geared to appeal to an arty crowd, the place is refrigerator cool and the chilled beats match the hot cuisine perfectly. An ultra-sultry lounge next to the main dining area pulls the mixed young and beautiful crowd into its bedroom-like setting of pillars, mirrors and minimalism reminiscent of a bad New Romantics video. The set menu changes often, so you can go every night.

Not just coffee on offer . . .

EATING OUT

Best of the Rest

GRACHTEN-GORDEL EAST

CAFE AMERICAIN

ℹ️ Leidseplein 97

📞 624-5322

www.interconti.com/
netherlands/amsterdam/di
ning_amsame.html

🕐 7am–1am daily (non-guests welcome from 10am)

🚊 Trams 1, 2, 5, 6, 7, 10, 20

🍴 💶 – 💶

💳 Credit cards: AmEx, DC, M, V

Famed spy Mata Hari is rumoured to have held her wedding reception inside the art-deco walls of this Amsterdam institution. Today, theatrical types drop in for a pre-show meal before attending shows at nearby performance venues.

CAMP CAFE

ℹ️ Kerkstraat 45

📞 622-1506

🕐 8am–1am daily

🚊 Trams 1, 2, 5, 11

🍴 💶

💳 No credit cards

A sandwich stop for the mature gay man. Friendly staff and customers make it a nice place to rest your feet if you're in the neighbourhood.

LE MONDE

ℹ️ Rembrandtplein 6

📞 626-9922

🕐 8.30am–1am Mon–Thu & Sun; 8.30am–2am Fri–Sat

🚊 Trams 4, 9, 14, 20

🍴 💶 – 💶

💳 No credit cards

A late-night nosh spot for the gay clubbing crowd. The stumbling masses weave their way from the nearby discos to Le Monde till the small hours of the morning. Vegetarian options are available.

METZ

ℹ️ Keizersgracht 455

📞 520-7020

🕐 9.30am–5.30pm Mon–Sat, noon–5pm Sun

🚊 Trams 1, 2, 5

🍴 💶 – 💶

💳 Credit Cards V, MC, AmEx, DC, V, MC

If you've abused your credit cards on the famous department store's third floor, head upstairs to calm your nerves with a light lunch at the shop's in-store café. Even if it's just for a few moments, the wonderful view the café offers over Amsterdam should be enough to slow down your shopping spree.

PYGMALION

Nieuwe Spiegelstraat 5A

420-7022

11am–3pm Mon; 11am–10pm Tue–Sun

Trams 16, 24, 25

Credit cards: AmEx, DC, M, V

Chef Mathias Klaengeld whips up a changing menu of South African specialities, including roast zebra. The place is popular with the local gay folk, often crowded at lunchtime for the affordable and filling sandwich specials.

'T SWARTE SCHAEP

Korte Leidsedwars- straat 24

622-3021

noon–11pm daily

Trams 1, 2, 5, 6, 7, 10, 20

Credit cards: AmEx, DC, M, V

Dutch dining in a cosy 17th-century home. Why visit a museum when you can eat a meal in the real thing? No frills, just good, hearty food at the Black Sheep. Even royalty has been know to dine out at this Amsterdam institution

THE JORDAAN AND NORTHERN CANALS

BLAKE'S

Keizersgracht 384

530-2010

6.30–11pm Mon–Sat; Closed Sun

Trams 1, 2, 5

Credit cards: AmEx, DC, M, V

Zen-like dining in the minimalist restaurant of the fashionable hotel of the same name. Your heart rate may not be so zen-like when you get the bill, but the food is superb and probably worth the second mortgage.

CLAES CLAESZ

Egelantiersstraat 24–6

625-5306

6–11pm Tue–Sun; Closed Mon

Trams 7, 10, 17, 20

Credit cards: M, V

Sing-songs, close-knit tables and chaos provide the atmosphere: the kitchen provides the fondues. The place can get a little stuffy when crowded, but it's the Dutch cheese and cheesiness that will truly melt you.

COC CAFE

Rozenstraat 14

623-4079

9pm–midnight Tue– Thu & Sun; 10pm–4am Sat

Trams 13, 14, 17, 20

No credit cards

A friendly café/ sandwich bar run by Amsterdam's gay rights organisation, the COC. On Thursdays, proceeds go to groups and

Camp Cafe

EATING OUT

centres fighting HIV. Staff are friendly and very helpful if you have any questions about the scene. Pick up copies of any gay press you might need in the main entrance.

KOH-I-NOOR

ⓘ Westermarkt 29

☎ 623-3133

⏰ 5–11pm daily

🚊 Trams 13, 14, 17, 20

🍴 🚭 – 🍴

💳 Credit cards: AmEx, DC, M, V

One of the better places in the city to get a curry. Service and atmosphere give it the thumbs up.

OSAKA

ⓘ 12th Floor, Het Havengebouw, De Ruijterkade 7

☎ 638-9833

⏰ noon–11pm Mon–Fri; 5–11pm Sat & Sun

🚊 Trams 1, 2, 5, 11, 13, 17, 20

🍴 🚭

💳 Credit cards: AmEx, DC, M, V

Wow, look at the harbour! Wow, look at the prices! Probably the best Japanese restaurant in town, Osaka battles it out with Blake's for the wallets of Amsterdam's *sushi* and *teriyaki* fans. While Blake's gives you the interiors, you just can't beat

Osaka's incredible view.

TAPAS BAR A LA PLANCHA

ⓘ 1er Looiersdwarsstraat 15

☎ 420-3633

⏰ 2pm–1am Tue–Thu & Sun; 2pm–3am Fri & Sat; Closed Mon

🚊 Trams 1, 2, 5, 7, 10, 20

🍴 🚭

💳 Credit cards: M, V

The latest trend to hit Amsterdam, tapas bars are sprouting up all over the city. This place is generally acknowledged to be one of the better ones. It's also one of the only dining hotspots in town that encourages you to take your time. Enjoy.

THE OLD CENTRE: NEW SIDE

1E KLAS

ⓘ Centraal Station, Line 2B

☎ 625-0131

⏰ 2pm–1am Tue–Thu & Sun; 2pm–3am Fri & Sat; Closed Mon

🚊 Trams 1, 2, 4, 5, 9, 13, 16, 17, 20, 24, 25

🍴 🚭

💳 Credit cards: AmEx, DC, M, V

Hark back to the days of grand train travel in this 'lost glamour' art-

nouveau masterpiece in Centraal Station. The food isn't the best in the city, but if you close your eyes you can almost hear the past creep up on you. Either that or it's another junkie trying to pick your pocket.

AL'S PLAICE

ⓘ Nieuwendijk 10

☎ 427-4192

⏰ 5–10pm Mon & Sun; noon–10pm Wed–Sat; Closed Tue

🚊 Trams 1, 2, 4, 5, 9, 13, 16, 17, 20, 24, 25

🍴 🚭

💳 No credit cards

Homesick Brits should head down to Al's for the traditional fish n' chips, pasties and mushy peas. It's as good as any you've had before.

D'VLIFF VLIEGHEN

ⓘ Spuistraat 294–302

☎ 624-8369

⏰ 5:30pm–10pm daily

🚊 Trams 1, 2, 5, 13, 17, 20

🍴 🚭

💳 Credit cards: AmEx, DC, M, V

Snobby Dutch food at snobby Dutch prices. This place is desperately looking for a famous connection to Amsterdam's Golden Age with no luck as of yet. Until

Cafe Het Karbeel

neighbourhood gay restaurant as popular as it is. While the food is fine, it's the funny girl floorshows that keep you coming back for more.

THE OLD CENTRE: ZEEDIJK, RED-LIGHT DISTRICT AND WATERLOO LEIN

then, enjoy the rooms, themed as they are around famous people of Amsterdam's past.

SARANG MAS

- Damrak 44
- 622-2105
- noon–10.45pm daily
- Trams 1, 2, 5, 13, 17, 20
- Credit cards: AmEx, DC, M, V

Sarang Mas is an incongruous little find in the centre of the neon-streaked wasteland of the Damrak. Smack bang next to some of the tattiest storefronts in the city, this place dishes up pretty tasty Indonesian treats from its kitschy kitchen. The 'artwork' provides its own, somewhat dubious, touches to the atmosphere.

STEREO SUSHI

- Jonge Roelensteeg 4
- 777-3010
- 5pm–1am Mon–Thu; 5pm–3am Fri; noon–3am Sat & Sun
- Trams 4, 9, 14, 16, 20, 24, 25
- Credit cards: M, V

Affordable Japanese. Considering the sky-high prices charged by other *sushi* emporia in town, the offerings here are refreshingly well-priced. Good for a late bite after a night on the town.

'T SLUISJE

- Torensteeg 1
- 624-0813
- 6–11pm Wed–Sun; Closed Mon & Tue
- Trams 1, 2, 5, 7, 10, 20
- Credit cards: M, V

It's the popular drag shows that make this

CAFE CUBA

- Nieuwmarkt 3
- 627-4919
- noon–1am daily
- Trams 4, 9, 14, 16, 20, 24, 25
- No credit cards

Cuban dishes, cigars and interiors in a café that would make Fidel feel right at home.

CAFE HET KARBEEL

- Warmoesstraat 58
- 627-4995
- 9am–1am daily
- Trams 4, 9, 16, 24, 25
- Credit cards: AmEx, DC, M, V

Friendly, family-run establishment that makes great fondues and chicken satays. The views of the Red-Light District are amazing from its front window. Just try and tune out the barking dogs and children that seem to populate the place.

GERARD

📍 Gelderse Kade 23
📞 638-4338
🕐 5–11pm Mon & Wed–Sun; Closed Tue
🚊 Trams 4, 9, 16, 24, 25
🍴 🍷 – 🍷
💳 Credit cards: AmEx, DC, M, V

Gay-friendly establishment with an emphasis on French cuisine. The cosy interiors are popular with local pink diners.

LIME

📍 Zeedijk 104
📞 639-3020
🕐 5pm–1am Tue–Thu; 5pm–3am Fri; noon–3am Sat; noon–1am Sun; Closed Mon
🚊 Trams 4, 9, 14, 16, 20, 24, 25
🍴 🍷
💳 No credit cards

Sandwiches, soups and desserts in this trendy bar and eatery. One of the better places for a light bite in this somewhat down-at-heel neighbourhood.

NAM KEE

📍 Zeedijk 111–13
📞 624-3470
🕐 11.30am–midnight daily 🚊 Trams 4, 9, 14, 16, 20, 24, 25

🍴 🍷 – 🍷
💳 No credit cards

The best Chinese in the city, no question. Fish dishes are what they are known for. So good there has even been a book written about it.

TOM YAM

📍 Staalstraat 22
📞 622-9533
www.tomyam.nl
🕐 5–11pm Tue–Sat; Closed Sun & Mon
🚊 Trams 4, 9, 14, 20
🍴 🍷 – 🍷
💳 Credit cards: AmEx, DC, M, V

Asian fusion catering to a gay crowd. Modern interiors and a varied menu make dining a pleasure.

THE PIJP AND MUSEUM QUARTER

ALBINE

📍 Albert Cuypstraat 69
📞 675-5135
🕐 10.30am–10pm Tue–Sun; Closed Mon
🚊 Trams 16, 24, 25
🍴 🍷 – 🍷
💳 No credit cards

Quick Surinamese food. A great place after a day shopping in the Albert Cuypmarkt. Its location in the heart of ethnic

Amsterdam gives it a flavourful vibe.

BAGELS AND BEANS

📍 Ferdinand Bolstraat 70
📞 672-1610
🕐 8.30am–6pm Mon–Fri; 9.30am–6pm Sat; 10am–6pm Sun 🚊 Trams 16, 24, 25 🍴 🍷
💳 Credit cards: AmEx, DC, M, V

Huge breakfasts are dished up daily at this crowded café. The outdoor patio is often full, so arrive early for a slice of the action.

BRASSERIE VAN GOGH

📍 PC Hoofstraat 28
📞 No telephone
🕐 10am–11pm daily
🚊 Trams 2, 3, 5, 12, 20
🍴 🍷 – 🍷
💳 No credit cards

Gay-friendly spot on the chic designer shopping strip, PC Hoofstraat. Prices are slightly elevated, due to its central location on an exclusive street.

CAFE VERTIGO

📍 Vondelpark
📞 616-0611
🕐 11am–11pm daily
🚊 Trams 1, 3, 6, 12
🍴 🍷 – 🍷
💳 Credit cards: AmEx, DC, M, V

Within the Neder-lands Filmmuseum,

Cafe Vertigo offers sandwiches, soups, desserts and coffees with a superb view of Vondelpark. The menu changes to suit the celebrated film seasons.

CAMBODJA CITY

🛈 Albert Cuypstraat 58–60 📞 671-4930 ⏰ 5–10pm Tue–Sun; Closed Mon 🚊 Trams 16, 24, 25 🍴 🍷 – 🏷 💳 No credit cards

Simple meals and service add to the enjoyment of eating any of the Thai, Cambodian, Laotian or Vietnamese dishes on the menu. Unpretentious yet satisfying.

MANKIND

🛈 Weteringstraat 60 📞 638-4755 ⏰ 11am–1am Sun–Thu; 11am–2am Fri & Sat 🚊 Trams 6, 7, 10 🍴 🍷 💳 No credit cards

Toasties, sandwiches and nibbles are available throughout the day at this friendly, family-run establishment for the mature gay man. The view from the outdoor patio is very pleasant, making an afternoon stay a distinct possibility.

THE PLANTAGE AND THE OOST

B & W CAFE

🛈 Plantage Kerklaan 36 📞 422-8989 ⏰ 11am–11pm daily 🚊 Trams 6, 9, 14, 20 🍴 🍷 – 🏷 💳 Credit cards: AmEx, DC, M, V

Adored by media types, the B & W serves up good basics and veggie dishes. Live music is performed on most nights.

DE MAGERE BRUG

🛈 Amstel 81 📞 622-6502 ⏰ 11am–11pm daily 🚊 Trams 9, 14, 20 🍴 🏷 – 🏷 💳 Credit cards: AmEx, DC, M, V

Named after the bridge it overlooks, this spot celebrates the food that comes from Amsterdam's canals.

EAST OF EDEN

🛈 Linnaeusstraat 11 📞 665-0743 ⏰ 11am–1am Mon–Thu; 11am–3am Fri & Sat 🚊 Trams 6, 9, 10, 14 🍴 🍷 💳 No credit cards

A stylish bar with a young, mixed crowd. Snacks are simple, but the vibe is good.

JERUSALEM OF GOLD

🛈 Jodenbreestraat 148 📞 625-0923 ⏰ noon–11pm; Closed Jewish Holidays 🚊 Trams 9, 14, 20 🍴 🍷 – 🏷 💳 No credit cards

Simple Jewish food recommended by the staff at the Jewish Historical Museum. The meals are heavy, filling and kosher.

KILIMANJARO

🛈 Rapenburgerplein 6 📞 622-3485 ⏰ 5–10pm Tue–Sun; Closed Mon 🚊 Bus 22 🍴 🏷 💳 Credit cards: AmEx, DC, V

Pan-African cuisine with a patio that's full in summer. Friendly and relaxed, it's one of the only decent eateries in the area.

SOETERIJN

🛈 Linnaeusstraat 2 📞 568-8392 ⏰ 5–11pm Mon–Wed, Thu & Sat; 11am–3pm Tue & Fri 🚊 Trams 7, 9, 10, 14 🍴 🏷 💳 Credit cards: AmEx, M, V

By the Tropenmuseum, this quirky restaurant celebrates the cuisine of the Third World. Menus change often, depending on the whim of the chef.

RESTAURANT FINDER

African
Kilimanjaro   89
Pygmalion   85
Soeterijn   89

Breakfast Hotspots
Bagels and Beans
                  88
Gary's Muffins   81

Cafés
Brasserie Van Gogh
                  88
Cafe Vertigo   88
De Jaren   80
East of Eden   89
Lime   88
Metz   84

Chinese
Nam Kee   88
Tom Yam   88

Cuban
Cafe Cuba   87

Dutch
Cafe Het Karbeel 87
Claes Claesz   85
De Magere Brug   89
Pancake Bakery   82

Fish
Al's Plaice   86

French
Le Garage   80
Gerard   88

Gay Hotspots
Backstage   79
Camp Cafe   84
COC Cafe   85
Downtown   80
Getto   81
Hemelse Modder
                  82
Mankind   89
Le Monde   84
't Sluisje   87

Indian
Koh-I-Noor   86

Indonesian
Sarang Mas   87

International
B & W Cafe   89
Inez IPSC   82
The Supper Club
                  82
't Swarte Schaep 85

Japanese
Blake's   85
Osaka   86
Stereo Sushi   87

Jewish
Jerusalem of Gold
                  89

Landmarks
Cafe Americain   84
D'Vliff Vlieghen 86

South-East Asian
1E Klas   86
Cambodja City   89

Spanish
Tapas Bar A La
  Plancha   86

Surinamese
Albine   88

Canal side refreshments

Afternoons and Coffee spoons

Amsterdam is famous for its freewheeling attitude towards soft drugs and it's hard not to stumble your way down any given block without coming across a coffeeshop plying the stuff.

A few facts:
- The sale of soft drugs is not strictly legal. The coffeeshops take advantage of the various loopholes in the law by following some basic guidelines that keep the police off their backs and their customers satisfied.

- Don't enquire as to how the coffeeshops get hash and marijuana into their establishments.

- Hash or weed can only be purchased in amounts of five grams or less.

- Coffeeshops can stock up to 500 grams of soft drugs on their premises at any given time.

- Up to 30 grams of the smokable substance can be held by an individual on their person. Any more is asking for trouble.

- Steer clear of any establishment that has a reggae beat playing over the loudspeakers and any accoutrements harking back to hippie days. You're bound to be disappointed.

- Alcohol and a trip to the coffeeshop do not mix. The quality of Dutch smoke is potent and the combination of the two can be overwhelming.

- If you're feeling woozy, eat anything with sugar (as long as it's not a brownie).

- Muggings, threats or worse are likely to greet anyone making a purchase on the street.

- Hard drugs will not be tolerated by anyone. One of the main purposes of legalising soft drugs in the Netherlands was to focus attention on the trafficking and distribution of Class A narcotics. Harsh treatment can be expected by anyone found using anything other than hash or grass.

- Natives aren't all that fond of people who decide to take their non-cigarette smoking into the public domain. Most bars will kick you out if you light up. Ask before you bask is the general rule of thumb.

Five of the better establishments that welcome gay clientele include:

Barney's

- **🛈** Haarlemmerstraat 102
- **📞** 625-9761
- **⏱** Nov–Feb 8am–8pm daily; Mar–Oct 7am–8pm daily
- **🚊** Trams 13, 14, 17, 20
- **💳** No credit cards

Head to Barney's for their full–on breakfasts of grease sprinkled with a few rashers of bacon. Feel your arteries harden as you giggle your way through the acres of food before you. Brits will welcome the HP and brown sauces this poky little venue makes available. Vegetarian and vegan breakfasts are a speciality. If you're older than 20, you might want to steer clear, as Barney's does seem to attract a seriously young crowd.

Greenhouse

- **🛈** Oudezijds Voorburgwal 191
- **📞** 627-1739
- **⏱** 9am–1am Mon–Thu & Sun; 9am–3am Fri & Sat
- **🚊** Trams 4, 9, 14, 16, 20, 24, 25
- **💳** No credit cards

Connoisseurs of skunk flock to this temple of toking in the Red-Light District. If you've ever had any questions about the wacky weed, the staff here will know the answers. Winner of the High Times Cannabis Cup more times than anyone can remember, Greenhouse has the added benefit of a bar from which you can get alcohol (a rare treat in coffeeshops).

Greenhouse Effect

- **🛈** Warmoesstraat 53
- **📞** 623-7462
- **⏱** 9am–1am Mon–Thu & Sun; 9am–3am Fri & Sat
- **🚊** Trams 4, 9, 14, 16, 20, 24, 25
- **💳** No credit cards

Conveniently located in the buzzing heart of the Warmoesstraat gay village, the Greenhouse Effect makes for a nice stop if you're on the way to the Queen's Head, Getto, Argos or any of the other numerous gay bars in the area. Not strictly gay, the Greenhouse Effect does welcome a mixed clientele, but can get loaded with loud British lager louts if you're not careful. A DJ spins ambient vibes to go with the atmosphere in the attached hotel of the same name, which is also a great place to get an alcoholic beverage.

The Otherside

- **🛈** Reguliersdwaarstraat 6
- **📞** 421-1014
- **⏱** 8.30am–1am Mon–Thu & Sun;

8.30am–2am Fri & Sat
Trams 1, 2, 5
No credit cards

First the good news. There is a gay coffeeshop catering to a mostly gay crowd on the Reguliersdwaarstraat. The cakes and coffees are quite delicious. And the vibrant techno music is of a standard suitable for the discerning queer. Now for the bad news. The service is shockingly awful. The employees will barely look at you when you place your order. And if you ask for anything out of the ordinary (like an ice cube in your drink), then you should prepare yourself for a withering stare. Outdoor tables are snapped up by cute creatures of the night

whenever they become available, making it one of the cruisiest spots in town.

T-Boat

Near 143 Oudeschans
423-3799
11am–6pm Mon–Thu & Sun; 10am–midnight Fri & Sat
Trams 9, 14, 20
No credit cards

Catch some rays as you enter a haze in this coffeeshop located on the deck of a boat near the Waterlooplein. The ship may be rocking, but it probably won't be due to any waves. On brighter days, the views can be quite soothing. Sadly, at f25 per gram, the cost isn't. As the saying goes: you get what you pay for.

Amsterdam has it all

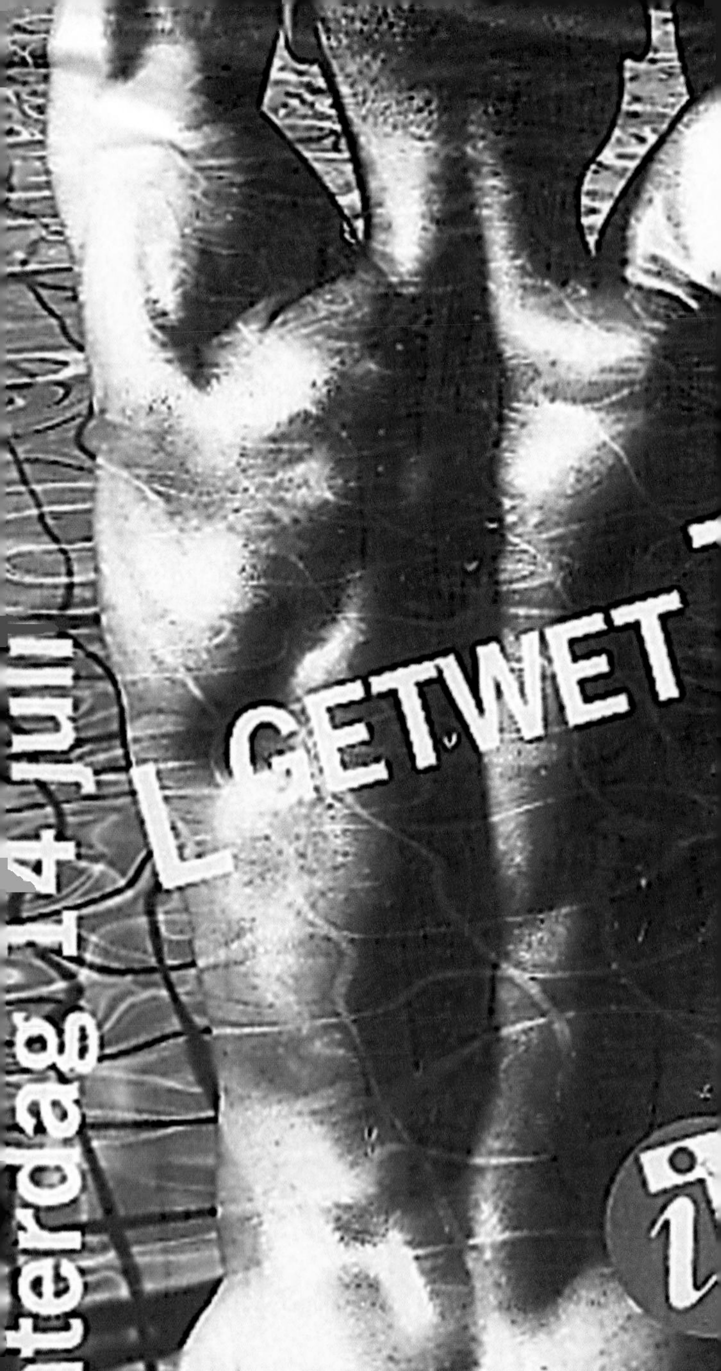

aterdag 14 Juli

L GETWET

i

Out on the Town

Clubs in Amsterdam tend to open and close rapidly. Nothing lasts forever, as the 1990s gay mega-club The Roxy proved when it burned down a few years ago. Closures are rife in the Dutch capital, often due to drugs offences, so always call ahead to ensure the place is still open. And don't forget the native custom of tipping the bouncer before you leave. If you don't, you can be sure they'll never let you back in ever again.

My Top Clubs

Amstel Taveerne

Amstel 54 623-4254 4pm–1am Mon–Thu & Sun; 4pm-2.45am Fri & Sat Trams 4, 9, 14, 16, 20, 24, 25 No credit cards

A typical gay brown café, with a popular pool table to draw the crowds. As with all other Amsterdam taverns, every glass of beer has the usual two inches of foam on top. This is a classic in the very essence of the word. Regulars, most of them older than 35, sink down at their usual stools on a daily basis to enjoy the hops and the happenings. No drag shows, no spectacle, no youngsters in crop tops, just good ol'-fashioned drinking. Oh! And the occasional Dutch singalong too (if the mood is right). Relax and stay awhile.

Argos

Warmoesstraat 95 622-6595 10pm–3am Mon–Thu & Sun; 10pm–4am Fri & Sat; Safe Sex Party at 3pm Sun Trams 4, 9, 16, 20, 24, 25 f10 (Sun only). No credit cards

If you've ever wanted to explore the basements of Amsterdam, then Argos is the place to go. Dark corners, an intense darkroom, a strict leather/denim/rubber dress code and a history going back to the 50s have made Argos a must-see on any leather man's list. Slings, chains, and secret passages provide the atmosphere. The last Sunday of every month is Sex on Sunday, an astronomically popular nude event that draws a large crowd. Doors open at 3pm and close promptly at 4pm. Men only.

Cockring

Men only

ℹ️ Warmoesstraat 96

📞 623-9604 www.clubcockring.com

🕐 11pm–4am Mon–Thu; 11pm–5am Fri and Sat

🚊 Trams 4, 9, 16, 20, 24, 25

💳 Varies. No credit cards

The sweat's dripping off you, the queue to get in was an hour long and you've just paid an outrageous f6 for a beer. You could only be in Cockring. The sex, the raunch, the pumping music and the boys make Cockring the most popular club in the city. Forty or under is the average age, with darkrooms, live sex shows, massages and raffles pulling in the punters.

Sex parties pack the place every second Sunday, while the first Wednesday of the month is underwear only. Don't forget to tip the doormen, otherwise you'll never get in again. Men only.

De Spyker

ℹ️ Kerkstraat 4 📞 620-5919 🕐 1pm–3am Mon–Thu; 1.30pm–4am Fri & Sat 🚊 Trams 1, 2, 5 💳 No credit cards

A campy leather bar that attracts a diverse crowd. This poky little place invites one and all into its dark and stormy interior. Cartoons and sporting events screen next to hardcore porn as drinkers jostle for turns on the billiard table. Young and old alike frequent this neighbourhood local, where the nights can be rollicking or rock bottom depending on the quality of the crowd. Rare for a leather bar, women are allowed to accompany their male friends. Wear combats, leathers or denim to fit in, but don't feel uncomfortable if you're dressed otherwise.

Exit

ℹ️ Reguliersdwarsstraat 42

📞 625-8788

🕐 11pm–4am Mon–Thu, Sun; 11pm–5am Fri & Sat

🚊 Trams 1, 2, 4, 5, 9, 14, 16, 20, 24, 25

💳 No credit cards

A favourite place to begin a night on the town, Exit is also well known for being the club of last resort. The bar in front is good for a bevvy, while the real party action goes on in the disco room. Fag hags are welcome (in small amounts), but the club is really geared towards a young, attractive, gay male crowd. Dress your best. Labels should be as visible as possible with much flashing of teeth, muscles and wallet expected.

De Spyker Bar

iT

🛈 Amstelstraat 24 | 📞 625-0111 | ☀ 11pm–4am Thu; 11pm–5am Fri & Sat; Closed Mon–Wed & Sun | 🚃 Trams 4, 9, 14 | 💳 No credit cards

The club of the past remains the hit of the present. Steeped in history, iT broke all bounds when it opened over a decade ago with its wild mix of drag, dancing, dope and dynamism. Now, a mostly suburban crowd queues up to capture a bit of the magic in hopes of reliving the days when celebs, stunners and sex gods packed the place to the rafters. Weekends are busy, with Saturdays remaining gay only. Thursdays are free if you can prove you're pink. Nights vary depending on who's decided to go, so make sure you have no expectations in order to avoid being disappointed.

OUT ON THE TOWN

Lellebel

ⓘ Utrechtsestraat 4 | ☎ 427-5139
| ⏰ May–Sep 9pm–3am Mon–Thu & Sun;
9pm–4am Fri & Sat; Oct–Apr 9pm–3am
Mon–Thu & Sun; 8pm–4am Fri & Sat
| 🚊 Trams 4, 9, 14 | 💳 No credit cards

Amsterdam's most popular trannie
shack, Lellebel is pure fun and
frivolity. Weekend evenings at 9pm
bring out the professionals as they
dance, lip-sync and cat-call to their
hearts' content. The girls can be
bitchy, brawny, brainy and brash,
but no matter who your hostess is
for the evening, you'll be sure to
have a good time. Wear whatever
you want and let your hair hang
out. I guarantee someone else there
will have plenty more of it to hang
out than you do.

Le Montmartre

ⓘ Halvemaansteeg 17
| ☎ 620-7622
| ⏰ 5pm–1am Mon–Thu; 5pm–3am Fri;
4pm–3am Sat; 4pm–3am Sun
| 🚊 Trams 4, 9, 14, 16, 20, 24, 25
| 💳 No credit cards

A postage-stamp sized dance-
floor and a bevy of young,
attitude-free cuties pack this
cheesy little bar festooned with
chilli lights, mirrored walls and
some of the most attractive
regulars near the Rembrandtplein.
A popular local, the bar is full
most nights with student types
and their admirers. It isn't cruisy
per se, but there's still a lot of
showing off among the party-
goers.

At the Tea Dance

MY TOP CLUBS

The bright lights

Why Not Bar/ Blue Boy Club

- Nieuwezijds Voorburgwal 28
- 627-4374 www.whynot.nl
- noon–2am daily
- Trams 1, 2, 5, 11, 13, 17,20
- Credit cards: AmEx, M, V

The oldest male brothel in the city, this House of Boys (as it likes to call itself) is a multi-storey arrangement of private rooms, two bars and a stage that exhibits live sex shows. Quiet drinks can be had in the bar downstairs, with many locals popping in for the casual, laid-back atmosphere and chatty nature of the employees. Upstairs, where the 'boys for sale' congregate (around three to five at any one time), the drinks rise in price. Some of the boys will try to go in for the kill as soon as you walk in the door, others wait for you to notice them. Most speak English and will discuss with you what they're willing to do for the f250 hourly fee. The owner states that all the boys have to be gay or bisexual, they all get check-ups every three months and they all must wear condoms.

If you want to get a taste of what it's all about, call ahead for details of their live sex shows.

Queen's Head

- Zeedijk 20
- 420-2475
- www.queenshead.nl
- 5pm–1am Mon–Thu; 5pm–3am Fri; 4pm–3am Sat; 4pm–1am Sun
- Trams 4, 9, 16, 20, 24, 25
- No credit cards

The Queen's Head welcomes any and all into its multi-coloured interior. Tuesday nights see co-owner Dusty the drag queen spinning her balls around for a crazy round of bingo. Locals drop by to win one of the prizes 'elegantly' wrapped in a plastic handbag even your mother wouldn't touch. If you're a collector of Billy dolls, take a peek at the walls – the owners have a complete set of the fantastic plastic gay figurine. The view out the back is one of the prettiest in the Red-Light District and gets crowded on Sportswear day (first Wednesday in the month). Wide-screen sports draws the crowds.

All Clubbed Out

APRIL

ℹ️ Reguliersdwars-straat 37

📞 625-9572

🕐 2pm–1am Mon–Thu & Sun; 2pm–2am Fri & Sat

🚊 Trams 1, 2, 4, 5, 9, 14, 16, 20, 24, 25

💳 No credit cards

So hip it hurts. If you like crowds and conversation, then don't come here. Popular due to its location (and only due to its location), if the drink prices don't kill you then the revolving stage will. Service is the worst in town and the place doesn't even start to get remotely busy until well after 11pm.

BACKDOOR

ℹ️ Amstelstraat 32

📞 06-21200922

www.backdoor.nl

🕐 Winter 6pm–1am; Summer 8pm–2am Sun only

🚊 Trams 4, 9, 14

💳 No credit cards

The weekly Sunday tea-dance at the Backdoor may only have been going since 1999, but it's already an institution among the locals. Chart hits pump over the speakers as the buffed-up boys and girls dance till they drop on the large (for Amsterdam) central floor. The place is divided in two, with a chilled out bar/ couch area on your left as you come in and a dance floor surrounded by over-stuffed Victorian-style couches on the right. Drinks are pricey, but what would you expect in a place as hot as this?

BOYS' CLUB 21

ℹ️ Spuistraat 21

📞 622-8828

🕐 noon–2am daily

🚊 Trams 1, 2, 5, 11, 13, 17, 20

💳 Credit cards: AmEx, M, V

Amsterdam's 'other' male brothel, Boys' Club 21 is a hop, skip and jump from the Why Not down the street. Less popular and with fewer guys to choose from, the place is also less intimidating and friendlier. A straight team of brothers run the Boys' Club 21, making the place a bit surreal when you come to think about it. Sex shows are supposed to be on offer, but they were shut down due to a lack of quality men available when I visited the place. Prices are exactly the same as the Why Not.

CLUB TRASH

ℹ Location changes monthly. Information available at all good leather venues and shops.

🌐 www.gayamsterdam.net/trash

🎉 Sex party third Sat of every month

Hardcore leather action at a constantly changing venue. Check for details at any good leather store or club. Strict leather/rubber/fetish/gender codes make the place impossible to get into for women and curious types.

CLUB BPM

ℹ Rembrandtplein 17

📞 625-1329

🎉 11pm–4am Wed

🚊 Trams 4, 9, 14

💳 f15. No credit cards

Battling it out with More as *the* place to go to on a Wednesday evening, BPM is a wild, hard party geared to attract a wild, hard crowd. Shirtless and sexed-up is the name of the game. Arrive after midnight or you'll be waiting for signs of human life for a while.

COC

ℹ Rozenstraat 14

📞 623-4079

🎉 10pm–4am Fri. Bi-monthly leather nights. Sat women only

🚊 Trams 13, 14, 17, 20

💳 No credit cards

Home to the city's gay rights advocate, the COC holds regular parties for different social groups in and around the city. Women-only Saturdays are a popular favourite among the lesbian set, while Fridays are popular for all and sundry. Drop by the COC for a complete listing of what's coming up.

COSMO BAR

ℹ Kerkstraat 42

📞 624-8074

🎉 1pm–3am Mon–Thu; 1.30pm–4am Fri & Sat; Closed Sun

🚊 Trams 1, 2, 5

💳 Credit cards: AmEx, DC, M, V

A late-night bar that fills up after the clubs have closed. Customers tend to be mostly on the pull or desperate by the time they arrive here. You decide.

THE CUCKOO'S NEST

ℹ NZ Kolk 6

📞 627-1752

🎉 1pm–1am Sun–Thu, 1pm–2am Fri & Sat

🚊 Trams 1, 2, 5, 11, 13, 17, 20

💳 No credit cards

Men-only leather bar that reputedly has the best darkroom in the city. Due to its early opening hours, the Cuckoo's Nest tends to attract a large after-work and lunchtime crowd.

DE TRUT

ℹ Bilderdijkstraat 165

📞 No phone

🎉 11pm–4am Sun

🚊 Trams 3, 7, 12, 17

💳 f2.50. No credit cards

One of the city's many leather bars

OUT ON THE TOWN

Ask any young gay boy what the best club in the city is and chances are he'll say De Trut. Off the map, location-wise, De Trut is a bitch to get to and a bitch to leave. The place is wild, wacky and wonderful, with good music, cheap drinks and great attitude-free pick-up potential in the form of young students up for a laugh. Okay, the surroundings aren't all that conducive to safety (the club night is held in an old industrial complex), but you'll feel great knowing that all proceeds go to gay charities and organisations. Arrive early, as the doors shut as soon as the place is full. This can take as little as ten minutes. No straights allowed!

HAVANA

ℹ️ Reguliersdwarsstraat 17–19
📞 620-6788
🕐 4pm–2.30am Mon–Thu; 4pm–2.30am Fri; 2pm–2.30am Sat; 2pm–1am Sun
🚊 Trams 1, 2, 5, 16, 20, 24, 25
💳 No credit cards

Another Reguliersdwarsstraat watering hole, Havana is friendlier than most others on this souped-up street. Special events, like musical theatre evenings and grooved-down R&B dance sessions, are what makes this bar a winner.

MORE

ℹ️ Rozengracht 133
📞 No phone
🕐 11pm–4am Wed
🚊 Trams 13, 14, 17, 20
💳 f15–25. No credit cards

Wednesdays bring 'LIFE' to More, a special evening geared towards gays, with a mix of house, techno and ambient chart stuff spinning from the speakers. Draws a mixed crowd of scene queens and everyday Joes with a dash of the usual student crowd thrown in for good measure.

SAAREIN

ℹ️ Elandsstraat 119
📞 623-4901
🕐 5pm–1am Tue–Thu & Sun; 5pm–2am Fri & Sat; Closed Sun
🚊 Trams 7, 10
💳 No credit cards

Amsterdam's best-known lipstick lesbian bar, the place is now open to one and all after a recent refit. Despite the changes, the bar remains mostly for women, yet welcoming to their gay friends.

SHOWTIME

ℹ️ Halvemaansteeg 10
📞 620-0171
🕐 2pm–1am Sun–Thu; 2pm–3am Fri & Sat
🚊 Trams 4, 9, 14
💳 No credit cards

The newest bar in the Rembrandtplein area, Showtime promises to introduce poetry, theatre, live performance and much else to the gay scene.

SOHO

ℹ️ Reguliersdwarsstraat 36
📞 330-4400
🕐 8pm–3am Mon–Thu; 8pm–4am Fri & Sat; 4pm–3am Sun
🚊 Trams 1, 2, 4, 5, 9, 14, 16, 20, 24, 25
💳 No credit cards

A British-style pub, Soho is one of the more popular bars on the strip, offering a great Midnight Hour 2-for-1 to late-night boozers. Worth it but highly cruisy.

THE WEB

ℹ️ Sint Jacobsstraat
📞 623-6758
🕐 2pm–1am Mon–Thu & Sun; 2pm–2.30am Fri & Sat
🚊 Trams 1, 2, 3, 5
💳 No credit cards

Leather bar with dark-room, pool table, DJ and hardcore porn. Wednesdays are lottery night. Men only.

Heading for a night out

Parties and Festivals

Spring

The biggest party of the year happens on Queen's Day, 30 April, when the entire population of the Netherlands sheds its inhibitions in celebration of Queen Beatrix's birthday. No one actually cares how old the gay icon is, choosing instead to jam the streets with street vendors selling souvenirs in every shade of orange you can imagine. An outdoor stage is erected near the Homomonument, featuring a variety of local acts and DJs, but it's the open-air party on the Reguliersdwarsstraat that really makes Amsterdam the place to be to celebrate Queen Bea. Speakers are drawn from every bar in the vicinity as a central DJ plays every stomping techno, ambient, house and garage groove you can think of. Book your trip today.

Less than a week later brings Remembrance Day on 4 May. Honouring gays and lesbians who perished in World War II, the COC arranges a memorial service and performance at the Homomonument in conjunc-tion with the following day's Liberation Day party that celebrates the victory over Nazi Germany.

AIDS Memorial Day occurs on the last Saturday of May at the Beurs van Berlage. Names are read, candles are lit and a walk to the Dam takes place, keeping those memories alive.

Celebrating Queen's Day

Summer

Utrecht's Midsummer Canal Party is gay pride 'wet' style, held on a three-day weekend as close to 21 June as possible. Performances and parties keep the action going till very late, with one catch; everything, including the stage, is on water.

The civic-minded Dutch share their national Gay Pride honours by changing the host city of the annual pink party held on the last Saturday of June. Coinciding with this special day is Amsterdam Diners, a huge celeb-studded bash held to raise money for AIDS charities. Check the website www.aidsfonds.nl for info.

Amsterdam Pride, held on the first weekend of August,

is probably the biggest hangover generator in the city's festival calendar. More gay boys phone in sick the day after this three-day hedonism fest than at any other time of the year. Street parties and canal boat capers round off the excitement.

For pure glitz and glamour, check out the Hollywood Party held every August at iT. This is the night when the faded glory of the mega club is guaranteed to revisit for one night only.

Autumn

Leather Pride at the end of October is a ten-day event of parties, performances and events dedicated to lovers of leather. Local leather/rubber bars and shops often sponsor courses introducing newcomers to the world of fetish and leatherwear, so if you've ever been intrigued, then now is the time to try it out.

Check out the website www.leatherpride.nl for further details.

Winter

As with every other city in the world, 1 December is World AIDS Day.

The Homomonument is the place to be as locals, straight and gay, come out in a nationwide show of strength to remember the losses and fight back against this killer disease.

Leather pride

Ready to entertain you

Playing Around Town

Amsterdam has a lively cultural scene with world-renowned musicians and internationally recognised dance companies calling the city home. Theatre and opera can be a little on the weak side, but visiting companies and performers keep Amsterdam on the map.

Many of the more recognised companies and venues work on a subscription format, often selling out tickets well in advance. The Amsterdam Tourist Board can keep you up to date on forthcoming concerts, performances and gigs through their information line (0900-400-4040). Otherwise, give the AUB Ticketshop a call to see if there's anything available. Bookings can be made with a credit card on 0900-0191.

OUTLINES

ARENA
ℹ️ Boulevard 1
☎️ 311-1333
www.amsterdamarena.nl
🎭 Varies
Ⓜ️ Metro Bijlmer
🚫 No credit cards

The biggest venue in town. If a big name act is coming to Amsterdam then they'll be playing here. The usual asking price for a ticket is somewhere between f40 and f60, but of course it all depends on who's doing the performing.

BEURS VAN BERLAGE
ℹ️ Damrak 213
☎️ 627-0466
🎭 Box office: 2.30–5pm Tue–Fri; 12.30–5pm Sat; Closed Sun. Box office also opens 75 minutes prior to every performance
Ⓜ️ Trams 4, 9, 14, 16, 20, 24, 25
🚫 No credit cards

The home of the Nederlands Philharmonic and the Nederlands Chamber Orchestra, the cultural centre is a bit of a monstrosity with poor views and less than ideal sound quality. Still, the price can be right if you want a good evening out.

BIMHUIS
ℹ️ Oudeschans 73–77
☎️ 623-3373/box office 623-1361 www.bimhuis.nl
🎭 8–11pm on performance nights only
Ⓜ️ Trams 9, 14, 20
🚫 No credit cards

A temple to the world of jazz. Fans from around the globe come to worship both the venue and the various big and small names that bestow

Concertgebouw

their god-like presence on the hallowed stage. Tickets can be like gold dust, so arrive early or pick them up at the Amsterdam Tourist Board in advance. The venue is set to move in 2002 so check the website for updates.

CASABLANCA

ℹ Zeedijk 26
📞 625-5685
🕐 8pm–2am Mon–Thu & Sun; 10pm–4am Fri & Sat
🚊 Trams 4, 9, 16, 20, 24, 25
💳 Free

Twenty years ago, a night at the Casablanca could have seen Chet Baker, along with the rest of the junkie jazzers who called Amsterdam home, performing legendary gigs in the middle of their hunt for another fix. Today, even though

karaoke reigns supreme on weekends, a bit of the old brass magic comes back Sundays to Wednesdays. If you close your eyes, you can almost feel the legendary trumpeter's presence.

CONCERTGEBOUW

ℹ Concertgebouwplein 2–6
📞 Box office 671-8345
🕐 Box office: 10am–7pm daily
🚊 Trams 2, 3, 5, 12, 16, 20
💳 Credit cards: AmEx, DC, M, V

A favourite venue among the world's classical music elite, soloists, orchestras, conductors and the general public praise the venue's near-perfect acoustics. Ticket prices can be surprisingly affordable

or outrageously high, depending on who's on the bill for that evening. Summer concerts throughout July and August bring the ticket prices down, yet still invite some of the biggest names in the business.

KONINKLIJK THEATER CARRE

ℹ Amstel 115–25
📞 622-5225
🕐 Box office: 10am–7pm Mon–Sat; 1–7pm Sun
🚊 Trams 4, 6, 7, 10, 20
💳 Credit cards: AmEx, DC, M, V

A large-scale venue for visiting companies and mega-musicals. Everything from *Cats* to the Kirov Ballet performs here when they're in town.

MELKWEG

ℹ Lijnbaansgracht 234A
📞 531-8181
www.melkweg.nl
🕐 Box office: 5pm Mon–Fri; 4–6pm Sat, Sun & 7.30pm (start of each performance)
🚊 Trams 1, 2, 5, 6, 7, 10, 20
💳 No credit cards

A multi-discipline venue that hosts both experimental work from big-name artists and new projects from youngsters on the arts scene. The stage has seen a number of star dancers and choreo-graphers at the very beginning of their careers. Many times they return later on to thank the place for giving them their big break.

MUSIKTHEATER

🛈 Waterlooplein 22

📞 625-5455

☼ Box office: 10am–6pm Mon–Sat, 11.30am–6pm Sun

🚋 Trams 9, 14, 20

💳 Credit cards: AmEx, DC, M, V

A large and spacious performance venue that the Nationale Ballet and Nederlands Opera call home. Usually the place to find ambitious, exciting and large opera and dance.

PARADISO

🛈 Weteringschans 6–8

📞 626-4521

www.paradiso.nl

☼ Times vary

🚋 Trams 1, 2, 5, 6, 7, 10, 20 💳 No credit cards

A former hippie hangout, the Paradiso attracts everything from folk to hard rock onto its stage. The Rolling Stones once played here, so you never know what you're going to get.

VONDELPARK

🛈 Vondelpark

🎭 Open-air theatre 673-1499 ☼ Dawn–dusk daily

🚋 Trams 1, 2, 3, 5, 6, 12, 20 💳 No credit cards

On summer evenings, the open-air performances of theatre, music and dance in Vondelpark can be the perfect end to a beautiful day in this beautiful city. Wade your way through the buskers to see what's on by checking out the posters and leaflets plastered all over the park.

Paradiso

Try pedal power . . .

Working Out

Due to the premium on space in Amsterdam, health clubs tend to be small and ill equipped. Serious gym-bunnies should avoid public facilities, which are often inadequate and far outside of town. Those looking to keep trim are advised to check out Splash, the only centrally located gym suitable for serious workouts. As befits a town of its reputation, the sauna scene is large, with the Thermos chain ruling the roost. Packed crowds aren't unknown, so be sure to arrive early to avoid disappointment.

OUTLINES

AMSTELPARK
- Koenenkade 8
- 301-0700
- 8am–11pm daily
- Buses 170, 171, 172
- f35/hr. Credit cards: AmEx, DC, M, V

Forty-two tennis courts are available here, both indoors and outdoors. Rackets are available for hire if you're in a light packer.

BOOMERANG
- Heintjehoek Steeg 8
- 622-6162
- 9am–11pm daily
- Trams 4, 9, 16, 24, 25
- f25. Credit cards: M, V

New to the sauna scene, yet popular with a young crowd, the facilities are smaller than Thermos, yet infinitely friendlier. Good if you're in the Red-Light District and need a steam.

FLEVOPARKBAD
- Zeeburgerdijk 630
- 692-5030
- May–Sep 10am–5.30pm (or 7pm depending on weather conditions)
- Tram 14
- f4.75. No credit cards

Amsterdam's only outdoor pool within easy striking distance from the city centre. The children can get annoying.

MANDATE
- Prinsengracht 715
- 625-4100
- 11am–10pm Mon–Thu; noon–6pm Sat; 2–6pm Sun
- Trams 1, 2, 5, 11
- f25 for a day pass. Credit cards: M, V

Straight father-and-son team Rob and Robin run this friendly gay-only gym, centrally located just off the Leidsestraat. The place is a bit run down and doesn't have all the latest gadgets, but it does have the essentials in addition to regular aerobics classes. Attitude-free and lacking the posing you'd expect from a gay gym, it's a nice, casual place for a workout.

WORKING OUT

Take a dip . . .

RENT-A-SKATE

- ℹ️ Vondelpark 7
- 📞 06-5466-2262
- ☀️ Apr–Oct
11am–9.30pm Mon–Fri;
10.30am–8pm Sat & Sun
- 🚋 Trams 1, 2, 3, 5, 6, 12, 20
- 💳 f7.50/hr. No credit cards

If you're looking to see the Vondelpark at a faster pace than normal, rent a pair of blades from either of the two locations of Rent-a-Skate located in the park's premises. Friday nights are dedicated to the wheeled set as Vondelpark's paths are taken over by skaters. Pedestrians be warned.

SPLASH

- ℹ️ Looiersgracht 26–30
- 📞 624-8404
- ☀️ 7am–midnight daily
- 🚋 Trams 7, 10, 17, 20
- 💳 Day passes available for around f40. Credit cards: AmEx, DC, V

The biggest and most popular health club in the city, Splash is popular with the local gay crowd. A large selection of weights, classes and special treatments, including massage and personal training. No swimming pool, though. Shame really.

THERMOS BEACH

- ℹ️ Zuidstrand 5/on the Zandvoort Seashore
- 📞 573-0141
- ☀️ Summer only from dawn till dusk.
- 📞 Call for arrangements
- 💳 Credit cards: AmEx, DC, M, V

A gay, clothing-optional beach run by the people who own the Thermos sauna chain. Drinks, snacks and a nice pavilion are there to greet guests.

THERMOS DAY

| ℹ️ Raamstraat 33
| 📞 623-9158
www.thermos.nl
| 🕐 noon–11pm Mon–Fri; noon– 10pm Sat & Sun
| 🚃 Trams 1, 2, 5, 7, 10
| 💳 f30. Discounts for under 24s. Credit cards: AmEx, DC, M, V

The most popular sauna in the whole of Amsterdam, Thermos offers steam rooms, rest rooms, a bar, a swimming pool and hot tubs to the numerous clients who pass through its well-oiled doors. The place is clean and nicely maintained.

THERMOS NIGHT

| ℹ️ Kerkstraat 58–60
| 📞 623-4936
www.thermos.nl
| 🕐 11pm–8am Mon–Sat; 11pm–10am Sun
| 🚃 Trams 1, 2, 5
| 💳 f30. Discounts for under 24s. Credit cards: AmEx, DC, M, V

Same as above, only it's at night! Jammed at weekends, it has the additional facilities of a dark maze and cubby-holes.

ZUIDERBAD

| ℹ️ Hobbemastraat 26
| 📞 671-0287
| 🕐 Times vary
| 🚃 Trams 2, 16, 24, 25
| 💳 f4.75. No credit cards

Built in 1912, the Zuiderbad is one of the oldest indoor swimming pools in the Netherlands. Nude swimming on Sundays between 4 and 5pm.

... and sweat it out

Kijk Kubus – Rotterdam

Out of Town

Getting out of town is easy due to Holland's extensive rail network and its compactness. Day trips have been selected for their historical, architectural and political importance – like The Hague, home to the nation's parliament. Rotterdam, Holland's 'other' city, is highly recommended for those with a passion for fashion and modern design. Give it a whirl if you need a change of pace from the claustrophobia of Amsterdam. If shopping is your priority, then Delft should be at the top of your list. Fans of the locally produced blue-and-white porcelain may have to watch their wallets before entering the local potteries.

Delft

A picture-perfect sleepy little town, Delft is most famous for its delicate blue-and-white pottery. Replicas of the famous earthenware can be found in almost every souvenir shop in the country, each one detailed with windmills, peasants with clogs or clichéd canal scenes.

The town that sparked the initial craze is absolutely stunning in a typically Dutch kind of way. Dappled rivers flow past delicate cottages, while local farmers deliver their produce in horse-drawn wagons passing merchant houses that haven't been touched since the day they were built in the 17th century. The entire town looks like it could have stepped out of a Breughel painting. It is so utterly romantic, so perfectly charming that you almost have to pinch yourself that you haven't stepped back in time.

You can still see examples of the real Delft stuff being made at a few potteries in the city, one of the better ones being **De Delftse Pauw**. You won't find any bargains at the gift shops, though.

For historical examples of the town's pottery output, check out the **Museum Lambert van Meerten**. Strictly for fans of antiquities, the museum can be a blur of blue and white for those who don't get excited over acres and acres of pots and jars.

An unmissable stop in town is **Het Princenhof**. A former convent, it holds a vast collection dedicated to the life of Prince William of Orange. Assassinated at the home in 1584, you can still see the bullet holes that killed the Dutch royal icon. The beautifully lush grounds make for a nice stroll.

OUT OF TOWN

Finally, art lovers should take a side track to the village's Oude Kerk. Dating back to the 13th century, the church is most famous as the final resting place of Dutch painter Vermeer. Delft was a favourite painting spot for Vermeer, with many of his most famous works based on local scenes.

While there isn't much of gay interest in the area, Delft is still welcoming to queer couples. It's advisable not to be as open about your status as you would be in Amsterdam, as small-town attitudes still prevail. Don't worry about being too careful though, as no matter what you do, you're still in the Netherlands.

HOW TO GET THERE BY CAR
Delft is located about 60km away from Amsterdam to the southwest. Take the A4 out of town then change to the A13.

HOW TO GET THERE BY TRAIN
Trains run frequently from Centraal Station. The journey takes about an hour. You may have to change trains at The Hague.

DE DELFTSE PAUW
ℹ️ Delftweg 133 📞 015-212-4920 www.delftsepauw.com
🕐 Apr–Oct 9am–4.30pm daily; Nov–Mar 9am–4.30pm Mon–Fri; 11am–1pm Sat & Sun 💲 Free

Ubiquitous blue and white delftware

MUSEUM LAMBERT VAN MEERTEN
ℹ Oude Delft 199 **☎** 015-260-2358 **🕐** 10am–5pm Tue–Sat; 1–5pm Sun; Closed Mon **💳** f3.50. No credit cards

HET PRINCENHOF
ℹ Sint Agathaplein 1 **☎** 015-260-2358 **🕐** 10am–5pm Tue–Sat; 1–5pm Sun; Closed Mon **💳** f5. No credit cards

The Hague

Home to the nation's parliament, The Hague is chock-full of all things royal with buildings, throne rooms, museums and a wonderful art collection dedicated to the work of Dutch and Flemish masters.

Mauritshuis should be on the list of any visitor to the Dutch capital, with works by such notables as Rembrandt, Vermeer, Rubens and Van Dijk available to view. Like many other attractions in the city, the museum was once a stately home.

While The Hague is home to Queen Beatrix and her family, most of the royal residences remain closed to the public. You can still pass by the grounds of Huis ten Bosch Palace where Queen Bea spends most of her days, but you probably won't glimpse much.

For a whistle stop tour of the Netherlands, head on over to the miniature world that is **Madurodam**. Windmills spin, rivers flow and dams... well, they dam the entire nation in intricately small detail. Look closely and you might see a mini-you waving back.

Considering the size of the place, The Hague has a pretty large gay scene, with two bars and a dance club serving the locals. **Stairs** caters to the leather/denim crowd, while **Frenz** is more for the young set. And while it's nothing like the clubs and parties you'd find in Amsterdam, **Strass** provides a dance spot for gay Haguers to boogie the night away. Occasional drag shows liven up the otherwise conservative surroundings.

HOW TO GET THERE BY CAR
Take the A4 out of Amsterdam, changing onto the A44 when signposted. The Hague is about 50km south of the city.

HOW TO GET THERE BY TRAIN
Trains leave regularly from Centraal Station. The trip takes about 50 minutes and you might need to change trains at Leiden.

FRENZ
ℹ Kazernestraat 106 **☎** 070-363-6657 **🕐** 8pm–3am Thu–Sun; Closed Mon–Wed **💳** No credit cards

MADURODAM
ℹ George Maduroplein 1 **☎** 070-355-3900 www.madurodam.nl
🕐 Mar–Jun 9am–8pm daily; Jul–Aug 9am–11pm daily; Sep–Feb 9am–5pm daily
💳 f21. No credit cards

OUT OF TOWN

MAURITSHUIS
Korte Vijverberg 8 | 070-302-3456 www.mauritshuis.nl
10am–5pm Tue–Sat; 11am–5pm Sun; Closed Mon
f12.50. No credit cards

STAIRS
Nieuwe Schoolstraat 11a | 070-364-8191 | 10pm–2am Tue–Sat;
5pm–1am Sun; Closed Mon | No credit cards

STRASS
Balistraat 1 | 070-363-6522 | 10pm–5am Fri & Sat; Closed Sun–Thu
No credit cards

The Heart of the Hague – Binnenhof

Rotterdam

Poor Rotterdam. Always living in Amsterdam's shadow and often
overlooked because of it, Holland's second largest city is actually a
vibrant metropolis gaining stature in the international clubbing stakes
due to its urban grit and large warehouse spaces. Visiting DJs come to
town often as part of raver weekends, bringing the residents of this

otherwise working-class town out of their closets and into the streets.

Bombed heavily during World War II, the city centre was decimated by the time the liberating allies arrived, forcing residents to start from scratch to rebuild the place. The result is a *Blade Runner*-style skyline of modern buildings and exciting architecture that completely obliterates any vision of what the place might have looked like pre-1940.

Due to Rotterdam's designation as a European City of Culture for 2001, city planners have spruced the place up a bit. While the town is the location of one of the largest ports in the world, efforts are being made to make the waterfront a little more presentable than it has been in the past.

A symbol of Rotterdam's phoenix-like spirit is **Kijk-Kubus**, a set of quirky cube-shaped residences painted bright yellow and resting on stilts. You can see the buildings on almost any literature advertising the city and they're worth a gander up close. Number 70 is open for a look inside, should you want to do so.

Speaking of architecture, the **Nederlands Architecture Institute** is an excellent museum that examines the history of architecture as an art form and the basics behind urban planning. It's fascinating even for those with no knowledge of home design.

The best way to see Rotterdam's exciting skyline and urban rebirth is undoubtedly at the top of the 185-metre **Euromast**. It's a bit of a trek up, and quite deadly for anyone afraid of heights, but the views are really breathtaking.

Gay hotspots are plentiful as befits a city of this size, with information about happenings in the city available from any copy of *Gay Krant* distributed throughout Amsterdam and the Netherlands.

HOW TO GET THERE BY CAR
Go south from Amsterdam on the A4, then follow the A13. Rotterdam is about 73km away.

HOW TO GET THERE BY TRAIN
Trains leave directly from Centraal Station. The trip should take an hour, with no changes.

EUROMAST
Parkhaven 20 | 010-436-4811 www.euromast.nl
Apr–Jun & Sep 10am–7pm daily; Jul–Aug 10am–10.30pm daily; Oct–Mar 10am–5pm daily | f15.50. Credit cards: AmEx, DC, M, V

KIJK-KUBUS
Overblaak 70 | 010-414-2285 | 11am–5pm daily
f3.50. No credit cards

NEDERLANDS ARCHITECTURE INSTITUTE
Museumpark 25 | 010-440-1200 www.nai.nl
10am–9pm Tue; 10am–5pm Wed–Sat; 11am–5pm Sun; Closed Mon
f7.50. No credit cards

The Grand Krasnapolsky – rooms, restaurants and national monuments

Checking In

Unlike most other cities, hotels in Amsterdam tend to be small. Occupancy rates are very high, making bargains a rarity. Boutique hotels are the norm, with dozens of small-scale, personable rest stops. B&Bs are perfect for romantic getaways as they avoid the tour groups that pile into the 'big name' institutions. For name-dropping, Blakes is the place. Those on a budget may want to consider a hostel. You avoid the overcrowding and the price difference is often minimal.

The Best Beds

Black Tulip

ⓘ Geldersekade 16 *Geldersekade: map p. 40* ☏ 427-0933 www.blacktulip.nl ⊞
Trams 4, 9, 16, 20, 24, 25 ▢ ❷ – ❸ ▢ Credit cards: AmEx, DC, M, V

The Black Tulip offers the ultimate leather experience. A dream come true for the owner who opened the place in 1998, clients come back again and again for the meticulously designed rooms featuring slings, leather bindings, St Andrew's crosses and anything else a leather fetishist could dream of. Book well in advance, especially if the stay coincides with a major festival. Videos, leather gear and sexual aids are available to hire or buy for guests who have decided to pack light.

Blakes

ⓘ Keizersgracht 384 *Keizersgracht: map p. 28* ☏ 530-2010 www.slh.com/blakesham
⊞ 1, 2, 5 ▢ ❸ ▢ Credit cards: AmEx, DC, M. V

Designer Anoushka Hempel broke the mould when she opened this acclaimed boutique hotel in 1999. Luxury is the name of the game in this former theatre, with 26 individually designed rooms providing glamour, drama, elegance and refinement to the lives of the people who are lucky enough to get a reservation (there's another Blakes in London). Highly fashionable, rooms tend to be on the minimalist side with a modern flair. Sensational service and determinedly subtle staff top off the perfection.

The following price guides have been used for accommodation, per room per night

① = under f200

② = f200–f350

③ = over f350

The Golden Bear

ℹ️ Kerkstraat 37 *Kerkstraat: map p. 20* 📞 624-4785 www.goldenbear.nl 🚊 Trams 1, 2, 5 🏷️ **①** – **②** 💳 Credit cards: AmEx, DC, M, V

One of the most popular gay-only hotels in the city, the Golden Bear can be almost impossible to get into due to its high rate of repeat booking. Catering to the needs of a mostly mature gay crowd, the Golden Bear is high on the list of places to stay for bears and their admirers. Manager Theo is a friendly sort, welcoming one and all to his laid-back, well-appointed premises.

Frederik Park House

ℹ️ Frederiksplein 22 *Frederiksplein: map p. 20* 📞 420-7726 email: frederik.park.house@wxs.nl 🚊 Trams 6, 7, 10, 20 🏷️ **②** 💳 Credit cards: AmEx, M, V

An intimate, friendly guesthouse, the Frederik Park attracts a lot of long-stay guests who enjoy the huge rooms and laissez-faire attitude of the owners. It's a little bit out of the way if you're looking to be in the thick of the gay action. It attracts a mixed clientele.

The Black Tulip – one for lovers of leather

Hotel Kabul

ⓘ Warmoesstraat 38–42 *Warmoesstraat: map p. 44* **📞** 623-7158 **🚋** Trams 4, 9, 14, 16, 20, 24, 25 **💰 ①** – **②** **💳** Credit cards: AmEx, DC, M, V

Those on a strict budget should consider a stay at the cheap and cheerful Hotel Kabul. More a hostel than a hotel, the Kabul offers everything from dormitory beds to private rooms at very reasonable prices. Rooms are clean, if a little on the dark side, but the ultra-friendly staff will go out of their way to make your stay as comfortable as possible. A great location on the Warmoesstraat makes the Kabul worth a chance. Note: if you're looking for a gay-specific hotel then this is not the place to go.

Cheap and cheerful accommodation

Maes Bed and Breakfast

ⓘ Herenstraat 26 *Herenstraat: p. 28* **📞** 427-5165 www.xs4all.nl/~maesbb94 **🚋** Trams 1, 2, 5, 11, 13, 17, 20 **💰 ①** – **②** **💳** Credit cards: AmEx, DC, M, V

The gay Russian/American couple that own this elegantly appointed guesthouse on one of the prettiest streets in the Northern Canals greet their guests with an authenticity that is both personal and touching.

CHECKING IN

Rooms are nicely decorated without being over the top, providing an intimacy that is perfect for a short stay or a romantic break for two. Both straights and gays are welcome to reside in any of the sizeable rooms on the premises. The front room is the most elegant of all of the options, but it might not be for light sleepers, as the road out front can get busy. Low ceilings and a steep climb make the rooftop apartment a no-go for tall patrons. Cats and a no-smoking policy are the only things that might irk clients in this otherwise perfect place to rest your head.

Prinsen Hotel

ⓘ Vondelstraat 36–38 *Vondelstraat: map p. 52* 🕿 616-2323 Ⓜ Trams 1, 2, 3, 5, 6, 12, 20 💶 ❷ – ❸ . 💳 Credit cards: AmEx, DC, M, V

A three-star hotel with simple features and friendly staff. Rare for a hotel of this size, a lift is available for patrons who require easier access. Museum lovers will appreciate the convenience of the quiet location, a mere stone's throw away from the Rijksmuseum and the Museum Quarter. Furnishings are basic. Make sure to request a room that's not on the ground floor to avoid a sense of claustrophobia. And if you have a bad back, the too-soft beds could play havoc with your vacation.

Favoured for its location

The Pulitzer

ℹ Prinsengracht 315-31 *Prinsengracht:
map p. 20*
✆ 523-5235 www.sheraton.com
🚊 Trams 13, 14, 17, 20
Ⓔ Ⓔ
💳 Credit cards: AmEx, DC, M, V

If you're a fan of American chain
hotels, then the Pulitzer is for you.
A little more intimate and welcoming than you might expect from a
Sheraton property, the Pulitzer
hosts a number of events and
festivals celebrating everything
from flowers to wine at various
times throughout the year. The
place can get overrun with huge
tourist block-bookings, so you
might want to avoid it if there's a
big convention in town. A restaurant of the same name located on
the premises is a wonderful locale
for breakfast or coffee.

Stablemaster Hotel

ℹ Warmoesstraat 23 *Warmoesstraat:
map p. 44*
✆ 625-0148 **🚊** Trams 4, 9, 16, 24, 25
Ⓔ Ⓔ
💳 Credit cards: AmEx, DC, M, V

The owner's unfriendly, the staff
gruff and unhelpful. No tourist
information is available or
forthcoming and the place is
generally pretty divey-looking for
the price.

So why do patrons flock back
to the Stablemaster? Location,
location, location. Slap bang in
the middle of the leather district,
the Stablemaster is one of the
most convenient places to rest
your head in the Red-Light
District. Nightly Jack-Off Parties
pack the downstairs bar, with
residents getting first crack at
admission.

Westend

ℹ Kerkstraat 42 *Kerkstraat: map p. 20* **✆** 624-8074 **🚊** Trams 1, 2, 5
Ⓔ Ⓔ **💳** Credit cards: AmEx, DC, M, V

Owners Remco and Johan have transformed the Westend into a
positive jewel of a place following considerable renovations. Modern
art and Ikea-esque furniture appeal to the young, hip and sexy
patrons who call this place home. Not all the rooms have en-suite
bathrooms so make sure you confirm your room's amenities before
you book.

The place may be changing its name to the Hotel Amistad by the
time you read this guide, so don't be shocked if there's a new sign on
the door when you check in. Watch your back around Remco
though, as he is definitely the biggest flirt in the Amsterdam hotel
business. But trust me, with his looks, you won't mind one bit.

Hotels and other attractions in Kerkstraat

AERO HOTEL

🛈 Kerkstraat 49

📞 622-7728

www.aerohotel.nl

🛏 Trams 1, 2, 5

🛏 ① – ②

💳 Credit cards: AmEx, M, V

Just above the Camp Cafe, the Aero Hotel is a budget property catering to a mixed-mature gay clientele. Check-in is done through the Camp Cafe and is thus only open during the restaurant's opening hours.

BARANGAY B&B

🛈 Droogbak 15

📞 777-9915

www.barangay.nl

🛏 Trams 1, 2, 5, 13, 17, 20

🛏 ① – ②

💳 Credit cards: AmEx, DC, M, V

A popular 17th-century guesthouse that once sat directly on Amsterdam's shoreline. Land reclamation has moved Barangay to drier land, but the picturesque property remains well located.

DRAKE'S GUESTHOUSE

🛈 Damrak 61

📞 638-2367

www.drakes.nl

🛏 Trams 4, 9, 16, 20, 24, 25

🛏 ① – ②

💳 Credit cards: AmEx, DC, M, V

A well-maintained, two-star property right on the Damrak, Drake's is owned and operated by the people who run the popular sex shop of the same name. There is no reception, so check-in arrangements must be made in advance. Guests receive free entrance into the often-crowded Drake's cinema broadcasting hardcore porn throughout the day.

FREELAND HOTEL

🛈 Marnixstraat 386

📞 622-7511

🛏 Trams 1, 2, 5

🛏 ① – ②

💳 Credit cards: AmEx, DC, M, V

A down-at-heel establishment located conveniently just off the Leidseplein. For the location, the price can't be beaten. You won't want to do more than sleep in its somewhat dusty rooms, though.

THE GRAND

🛈 Oudezijds Voorburgwal 197

📞 555-3111

www.thegrand.nl

🛏 Trams 4, 9, 14, 16, 20,

A picturesque place to stay

24, 25 | 🔵 **③**
| 💳 Credit cards: AmEx,
DC, M, V

The Grand originally
opened in the 16th
century as an inn.
Among its former
guests are Prince
William of Orange
and a host of inter-
national celebrities. A
great location if you
like the prestige of
five-star service
combined with a
sense of history.

GRAND HOTEL KRASNAPOLSKY

| ℹ️ Dam 9
| 📞 554-9111
www.goldentulip.com
| 🚊 Trams 1, 2, 4, 5, 9, 13,
14, 16, 17, 20, 24, 25
| 🔵 **③**
| 💳 Credit cards: AmEx,
DC, M, V

The best location of
any grand hotel in the
city, the Krasnapolsky
is part of the boutique-
styled Golden Tulip
chain of five-star
establishments. A wide
selection of highly
rated in-house
restaurants and two
national monuments
confirm its popularity.

HOTEL ANCO

| ℹ️ OZ Voorburgwal 55
| 📞 624 1126
www.ancohotel.nl
| 🚊 Trams 4, 9, 16, 20,
24, 25
| 🔵 **①** – **②**

| 💳 Credit cards: AmEx,
M, V

A leather hotel in
the heart of the Red-
Light District, the
Anco has been enter-
taining guests since
1962. Televisions and
videos are in each
room, yet individual
in-room phones
aren't. Queen's Day
bookings sell out a
year in advance to the
mostly leather crowd.
An attached bar is a
popular stop for both
non-guests and
residents.

SUNHEAD OF 1617

| ℹ️ Herengracht 152
| 📞 626-1809
www.sunhead.com
| 🚊 Trams 13, 14, 17, 20
| 🔵 **②**
| 💳 Credit cards: AmEx,
DC, M, V

A gorgeous B&B with
vaulted ceilings and
delightful owners,
the Sunhead of 1617
is a highly-rated place
for both straights
and gays
to rest
their
heads. The
breakfasts,
included
in the
price, are
mouth-
wateringly
good.

ITC HOTEL

| ℹ️ Prinsengracht 1051
| 📞 623-0230
| 🚊 Trams 4, 6, 7, 10
| 🔵 **①** – **②** .
| 💳 Credit cards: AmEx,
DC, M, V

A beautiful canal-side
house on one of the
most picturesque
streets in Amsterdam,
ITC is conveniently
located for much of
the gay action. The
pleasant combination
has proven to be a
hit with ITC's mixed
lesbian and gay
clientele.

ORFEO HOTEL

| ℹ️ Leidsekruisstraat 14
| 📞 623-1347
| 🚊 Trams 1, 2, 5, 6, 7, 10
| 🔵 **①**
| 💳 Credit cards: AmEx,
M, V

A somewhat bland
hotel on a non-
descript street, the
Orfeo remains
popular due to its
well-priced rooms.

**The following price
guides have been used
for accommodation,
per room per night**

① = under f200

② = f200–f350

③ = over f350

Wish you were here?

Check This Out

Any traveller needs to know the practical information about getting to the city, the day to day stuff and support available in the city. Not quite as interesting as what you are going to do when you get there, but it is essential reading before you set out and reference during your stay.

Getting There

BY AIR

Amsterdam is a major destination and gateway point for most international carriers travelling to Europe. The national flag carrier KLM operates flights to Amsterdam from destinations around globe. However, train travel is easy from all continental European destinations and is often the fastest and most convenient method of travel.

AER LINGUS
01-886 8888
www.flyaerlingus.com

AMERICAN
1-800-433-7300
www.im.aa.com

AIR CANADA
1-800-555-1212
www.aircanada.ca

BRITISH AIRWAYS
All enquiries 0345-222111
02/8904-8800 (Australia)
09/356 8980 (New Zealand)
www.britishairways.co.uk

BRITISH MIDLAND
All enquiries 01332-854000
www.flybmi.co.uk

CONTINENTAL
1-800-231-0856
www.continental.com

DELTA
1-800-241-4141
www.delta.com

EASYJET
All enquiries 0870-6000 000
www.easyjet.com

KLM
08705-074074 (UK)
www.klmuk.co.uk
1-300-303-747 (Australia)
www.klm.com

NORTHWEST
1-800-447-4747
www.nwa.com

UNITED
1-800-538-2929
www.ual.com

CHECK THIS OUT

SCHIPHOL INTERNATIONAL AIRPORT
ℹ️ 14 km southwest of the city centre
📞 0900 0141 www.schiphol.nl

The only gateway that serves the city. A modern, clean and efficient terminal greets all passengers with easy transport links to the downtown core.

Shuttle buses, taxis and trains all service the main arrivals concourse. KLM Hotel Bus Service, Main Exit, Schiphol Airport (653-4975) runs every 30 minutes between 6.30am and 3pm, then every hour until 10pm (f 17.50 single, f 30 return). Taking about 30 minutes to central Amsterdam, the KLM shuttle service operates door-to-door departures from Schiphol to most major hotels. You do not need to have been a KLM passenger to ride the shuttle. Schiphol Airport Rail Service, Schiphol Airport, Arrivals Level (0900-9292), every 15 minutes 4am–midnight, then every hour from 12.44am (f6.50).

The fastest way to reach central Amsterdam is by rail, with services taking 20 minutes to Centraal Station. Note that return tickets are only valid for same-day travel.

Taxis are available from outside the main entrance. The price is approximately f70 and the journey takes 20–30 minutes.

BY TRAIN

CENTRAAL STATION INFORMATION
ℹ️ Stationsplein 15 📞 0900-9292
🕐 Information desk 6.30am–10pm daily.
Reservations 24 hrs 🚊 Trams 1, 2, 4, 5, 9, 13, 16, 17, 20, 24, 25
💳 Credit cards: M, V

All international trains to Amsterdam wind up at Centraal Station. The station is located in the very centre of the city, with almost every tram service stopping outside the front doors.

The crime rate in the station is very high, so keep all belongings close at hand to prevent theft and pickpocketing. Don't let anyone help you with your luggage unless they are uniformed train staff.

BY BUS

EUROLINES
ℹ️ Rokin 10 📞 560-8787
www.eurolines.com 🕐 24 hrs
🚊 Trams 4, 9, 14, 16, 20, 24, 25
💳 Credit cards: M, V

All long-distance buses depart and arrive from the concourse outside Centraal Station next to Amstelstation. Eurolines is one of the better carriers.

PASSPORTS AND VISAS

Residents of the EU, Canada, Australia, the United States and New Zealand do not require a visa for any visit to the Netherlands.

Centraal Station

A valid passport is all that is required for a stay of up to three months. Other foreign nationals should apply for visas through the Dutch Embassy in their country of origin. Stays of longer than three months require a resident's permit (MVV visa) regardless of where you are coming from.

CUSTOMS

EU nationals over the age of 17 years may import limitless goods of a personal nature. Non-EU citizens may only bring in 200 cigarettes or 50 cigars or 250 grams of tobacco, 2 litres of non-sparkling wine plus one litre of spirits or 2 litres of fortified wine, 60ml of perfume and any other goods to a value of f 368.

The import of meat, meat products, fruits, plants, flowers and protected animals is forbidden. Check your local customs regulations regarding the import of tulip bulbs if you are planning on making any purchases.

HIV-positive travellers should have no problem entering the country and do not need to declare their status to any immigration officials.

In the City
TOURIST OFFICES AND INFORMATION

One of the best tourist boards in Europe, the Amsterdam Tourist

Lots to do, lots to see

Board can change money, provide free maps of the city, book entertainment and attraction tickets, arrange day trips and reserve hotel accommodation and car rental. All the staff speak fluent English and most will go out of their way to make your stay as enjoyable as possible. The main office is located directly outside Centraal Station.

AMSTERDAM TOURIST BOARD

ℹ️ Stationsplein 10. Other locations Leidseplein 1, Centraal Station, Schiphol Airport 📞 0900-400-4040

🕒 Stationsplein: 9am–5pm daily; Leidseplein: 9am–5pm daily; Centraal Station: 8am–8pm daily; Schiphol Airport: 7am–10pm daily

🚊 Trams 1, 2, 4, 5, 9, 13, 16, 17, 20, 24, 25

ACCOMMODATION

While all hotels may not give you the same level of satisfaction, they are all bound by law to treat gay guests with the same respect and tolerance as they would any other customer. Sharing a room with a partner is allowed, and the general attitude towards such a request is positive.

For gay-specific places to stay, the best bet is to ring or email the hotel or guesthouse to book your stay. Accommodation agencies in the city deal mainly with non-gay-specific hotels, concentrating on the bigger names. The Amsterdam Tourist Board can be a great resource if you're stuck, in addition to the main hotel bookings service for the country, the Nederlands Reserverings Centrum.

Lots of gay-friendly hotels

NEDERLANDS RESERVERINGS CENTRUM

- PO Box 404, 2260 AK Leidschendam
- 070-419-5500 www.hotelres.nl
- 9am–5.30pm Mon–Fri

PUBLIC TRANSPORT

Amsterdam is a compact and therefore highly walkable city, making your own two feet the easiest way of getting around.

TRAMS

The extensive tram system covers most of the city, running 6am– midnight Monday to Saturday and 7am–midnight on Sunday. Night buses replace the trams in the intervening times.

Hop on and get around town

Almost every tram and night bus ends up at Centraal Station. To find a stop, look for a yellow tram sign that details the name of the stop and the future route of the tram that you are waiting for. Night bus stops are signposted in black.

Maps of the system are usually available at each shelter or by picking one up from the GVB, Amsterdam's municipal transport authority.

Getting on or off the tram is easy. Wait until the tram has stopped and then press the yellow button to open the doors. Tickets can be purchased from the driver, or from a machine or conductor at the rear of the tram.

One of the cheapest and easiest ways to see the city is by riding Tram 20. Known as the 'Circle Line', Tram 20 passes by almost all of the major sites and is never very busy. There are discussions to terminate the route due to its unpopularity with locals, so keep your eyes peeled just in case.

METRO

There is also a Metro system that covers parts of the south and east of the city. The stops are few and far between, making it inconvenient and relatively unusable for a visitor. If you are staying outside of the city then you might want to check out if it covers anywhere near your location.

TICKETS

The Metro, buses and trams all use the same form of ticket. You can try getting away with not paying the fare, but the fine dished out by uniformed inspectors on their regular spot-checks is a steep f64.50.

The cheapest way to get around if you'll be using public transport often is to purchase a *strippenkarten*.

Tickets are purchased in strips of units from post offices, tobacconists and tourist boards throughout the city and must be stamped each time you board a bus, tram or subway.

Initially confusing, you just need to know that the city is divided up into five zones. Single-zone travel costs two units, two-zone travel costs three units and so on. An unlimited number of people can use one *strippenkarten* as long as you have enough units to cover the journey.

If anyone attempts to help you purchase a ticket at Centraal Station, don't give them any money. It's the oldest trick in the book for the local addicts to pocket your change and run.

TAXIS

Taxis aren't a very smart alternative to the excellent public transportation methods available, due to their crippling cost and small numbers.

The initial charge for any taxi is f4.80. If you see any more on the meter then tell the driver or get out of the cab. Drivers should be able to give you a good estimate of the cost of any trip before you embark and you shouldn't be shocked if the estimate is high. For the first 25km, the meter will be running at f 3.40/km, dropping to f 2.80/km thereafter.

Legally, you are not allowed to hail a taxi from the street, though everyone does it. Taxis congregate at taxi ranks, usually found outside main squares, tourist sites, transport centres and hotels.

Amsterdam's Central Taxi Control on 677-7777 is the number to call to arrange for a pick-up or register a complaint.

CLIMATE

The climate in Amsterdam can change at any time, most often deciding to rain at the most inopportune moment. May to August is the best time to plan a visit, with temperatures usually hovering around the 22°C mark. Summer nights can be chilly, requiring a light sweater or jacket to keep you going.

Winter brings rain and windy conditions off the North Sea, making the city unpleasant. You'll need to wrap up.

TELEPHONING

Dialling codes in Amsterdam are 020 area prefix followed by a 7-digit number. If you are calling Amsterdam from outside the Netherklands, dial the international access code, followed by 31 (the code for the Netherlands) then the full number, omitting the first zero (0) from the 020 code.

If you want to call internationally from the Netherlands, dial 00 followed by the country code, then the area code (omitting the first 0) and then the local number.

To make a phone call from Amsterdam, listen for the dial tone and dial the number, omitting the 020 if you are calling locally. The minimum amount you may put into a phone box is half a guilder.

INTERNATIONAL DIALLING CODES

Australia: 61;
New Zealand: 64;
Republic of Ireland: 353;
UK: 44;
US and Canada: 1

DIRECTORY ASSISTANCE
📞 0900-8008

INTERNATIONAL DIRECTORY ASSISTANCE
📞 0900-8418

EMBASSIES AND CONSULATES

All the embassies and consulates listed below can provide assistance with lost passports and emergencies. Lists of recommended English-speaking doctors and lawyers are available should you require them.

None of the embassies or consulates can forward you money or financial assistance should you become a victim of theft; however, they will attempt to assist you in any other way that they can.

AMERICAN CONSULATE GENERAL
ℹ️ Museumplein 19
📞 664-5661/679-0321
🕐 8.30am–noon Mon–Fri for US citizens and visa applications; Closed Sat & Sun
🚋 Trams 3, 5, 12, 16, 20

BRITISH CONSULATE GENERAL
ℹ️ Koningslaan 44
📞 676-4343 🕐 9am–noon, 2pm–3.30pm Mon–Fri for British citizens; 9am–noon for visa enquiries; Closed Sat & Sun 🚋 Tram 2

CANADIAN EMBASSY
ℹ️ Sophialaan 7, 2514 JP The Hague
📞 070-311-1600 🕐 10am–noon Mon–Fri; 2.30–4pm Mon, Tue, Thu & Fri for Canadian nationals; Closed Sat & Sun. Visa enquiries must be made via the consulate in Berlin.

Alternative transport

CHECK THIS OUT

NEW ZEALAND EMBASSY

ℹ️ Carnegielaan 10, 2517 KH The Hague

📞 070-346-9324

🕐 9am–12.30pm, 1.30–5pm Mon–Fri;
Closed Sat & Sun

REPUBLIC OF IRELAND EMBASSY

ℹ️ Dr Kuyperstraat 9, 2514 BA The Hague

📞 070-363-0993

🕐 10am–12.30pm, 2.30–5pm Mon–Fri;
Closed Sat & Sun

POLICE AND CRIME

In case of any emergency, ring ambulances, police and fire departments on 112. A gay section of the local police force is available and you can request a gay officer if you'd feel more comfortable dealing with a queer copper. The Politie is very supportive of the gay community, often cropping up at events and parties to give a show of strength.

Prostitution is legal in the Netherlands, with a few restrictions placed on the tax-paying 'men of the night'. All prostitutes are subject to a three-month check-up from an accredited doctor, and safe sex is a must. Clients are required to rubber-up. If you are given the choice of going condom-free, think twice before you make any moves. Chances are the boy you are dealing with is not following all the laws and could be exploited, HIV-positive or worse.

DRUGS

The Amsterdam police take a very relaxed stance on the use of soft drugs, including hash, marijuana, poppers and magic mushrooms. Individuals are allowed to carry up to 30g of the stuff on them at any given time. But, you should note that lighting up anywhere you want isn't *au fait* with the locals. Ask before you start smoking is the general etiquette.

Harder drugs will be strictly dealt with. This includes ecstasy, heroin, speed, LSD, crystal meth and cocaine. You will be prosecuted if you are found with any – and the resulting prison sentence and/or fine will be harsh. No embassy will be able to help you out of your jam if you are found in possession of, or under the influence of, any Class A narcotic.

SAFETY AND SECURITY

Other than the occasional pick-pocket, Amsterdam is a very safe city. Gay hate-crime is almost unheard of and the murder rate is negligible. Areas to avoid include Centraal Station (at all hours), the Zeedijk (pass by the dealers as quickly as possible), the Red-Light District (the volume of people makes this otherwise seedy area relatively safe) and the Leidseplein (drunken yobbos and wallet snatchers).

Walking at night should be fine, but you might want to consider a taxi if you're on the Warmoesstraat during the wee hours. The street isn't all that unsafe, but it can feel creepy late at night.

Centraal Station is where you'll find the bulk of the scams and petty thievery most annoying to travellers. Keep your belongings close at hand and don't talk to any of the junkies who hang out in the main entrance. There is a constant police presence in the main foyer to keep you feeling safe and warm.

HEALTH

As with all foreign travel, health insurance is recommended. EU citizens will be covered by the reciprocal agreements in effect. Form E111 is required by Britons, available at all DSS offices. Dutch medical costs are about half equivalent US prices. Vaccinations are not required to enter the Netherlands.

AFDELING INLICHTINGEN APOTHEKEN

😊 694-8709

😊 24-hour information on where to locate your nearest chemist/pharmacist

CENTRAAL DOKTORSDIENST/ATACOM

😊 592-3434

😊 English-speaking 24-hour information line for people who need advice regarding medical symptoms

TBB

😊 5709595

😊 The number to call if you need a dentist or have a dental crisis. Information about late-opening chemists is also provided by the helpful operators

HIV AND SAFE SEX

Refreshingly enough, HIV-positive travellers should find the Netherlands a joy to visit, with few obstacles impeding a pleasant journey. It is perfectly legal to bring HIV medication into the

Some soft drugs are legal here

Some great meeting places

country, and it is available from pharmacies in the city should you run out.

There are a number of groups that can help you with any problems you might face, including an AIDS Helpline (0800-022-2220, open 2–10pm Mon–Fri) that will direct you to the appropriate organisation or doctor.

HIV VERENING

- 1E Helmersstraat 17
- 616-0160
- 9am–5pm Mon–Fri; Closed Sat & Sun
- Trams 1, 2, 3, 5, 6, 12

An advocacy organisation that supports the legal interests of the HIV-positive community.

SCHORERFOUNDATION

- PC Hoofstraat 5
- 662-4206
- 9am–5pm Mon–Fri; Closed Sat & Sun
- Trams 2, 3, 5, 6, 7, 10, 12, 20

State-supported agency offering STD tests, HIV tests, information about physical and mental health and HIV prevention advice for gay men and lesbians.

STICHTING AIDS FONDS

- Keizersgracht 390
- 626-2669 www.aidefond.nl
- 9am–5pm Mon–Fri; Closed Sat & Sun
- Trams 1, 2, 5

The main funding body in the fight against AIDS. Organiser of countless fundraisers and bashes throughout Amsterdam, with all proceeds going to medical research and prevention campaigns.

GAY GROUPS AND RESOURCES

There are a number of gay groups catering to a variety of special interests throughout the city. A central meeting point that hosts many social groups is the COC. Check out their noticeboards for information on any new or upcoming group meetings that might interest you.

AMSTERDAM STETSONS

- 683-7333

http://people.a2000.nl/fokker/saloon/eng/saloon.html

Gay group for fans of country and western music. Line-dancing nights are often organised. Ring ahead for details.

BRIDGE-SOCIETEIT DE LOOIER

- Lijnbaansgracht 185
- 627-9380

Bridge courses and tournaments for gay men and lesbians.

COC AMSTERDAM

- Rozenstraat 14
- 626-3087
- Café 9pm–midnight Tue–Thu & Sun; 10pm–4am Fri & Sat: Discos 11pm–4am Fri & Sat: Phone enquiries 10am–5pm Mon–Fri; Coffeeshop 1–5pm Sat
- Trams 13, 14, 17, 20

Meeting place and information.

DIKKE MAATJES

- C/o COC Amsterdam
- 0343-531791

http://home.eu.org/~bigbear.nl

A club for big men. Chubs, bears and their admirers welcome.

CHECK THIS OUT

GAY GARDEN CLUB

ℹ️ Postbus 15672, 1001 ND

📞 688-1243

Garden visits and private home tours for gay men.

GAY AND LESBIAN SWITCHBOARD

ℹ️ Postbus 11573, 1001 GN

📞 623-6565 www.switchboard.nl

🕐 10am–10pm daily

If you need any information about the scene, including safe-sex guides, advice or a friendly voice, give this English-speaking organisation a call.

GAY SWIM AMSTERDAM

📞 625-2085

Weekly swimming for gay men.

HOMODOK

ℹ️ Nieuwpoortkade 2A

📞 606-0712 www.homodok-laa.nl

🕐 9.30am–4pm Mon–Fri; Closed Sat & Sun

🚋 Trams 10, 12, 14

Extensive collection of archives dedicated to the study of Dutch and international homosexuality. The location may be moving sometime in 2002.

LEATHER PRIDE NETHERLANDS

ℹ️ PO Box 2674, 1000 CR

📞 422-3737

www.leatherpride.nl

Organisers of the annual Leather Pride festivities in October, in addition to numerous other parties throughout the year.

Pink Point of Presence – information centre

LONG YANG CLUB HOLLAND
ℹ️ Postbus 58253, 1040 HG
📞 023-571-5788

A branch of the international organisation of Asian queers and their friends.

LOVE2LOVE
ℹ️ C/o COC 📞 626-3087

Social and advocacy group for lesbians and gay men under the age of 27. Special events are often planned to raise money.

NETHERBEARS
ℹ️ C/o Le Shako, Postbus 15495, 1001 ML 📞 625-1400
www.xs4all.nl/~elza/netherbears/club.htm

Hairy men's club that meets every second Sunday of each month.

SJALHOMO
ℹ️ Postbus 2536, 1000 CM Amsterdam
📞 023-531-2318
Evenings only

The national organisation for gay and lesbian Jews.

STICHTING IPOTH
ℹ️ Postbus 59564, 1040 LB
📞 684-2121

Events and parties geared towards gays and lesbians of colour. The centre has information on homosexuality and ethnicity. Safe-sex campaigns targeted at gay immigrants start from here.

SPORTCLUB TIJGERTJE
ℹ️ Postbus 10521, 1001 EM
📞 673-2458 www.xs4all.nl/~tijgertj

Outings, sporting events and activities for gay men and lesbians.

GAY LIFE IN THE CITY

Gay men and lesbians have the same rights as any other citizen in the Netherlands. There are no differences in access to employment, opportunity, marriage or adoption. The age of consent is . standardised for both gays and straights at 16.

Police, government and society attitudes towards homosexuality are very open and tolerant.

MEDIA

GAY PRESS
Good listings magazines to pick up include *Gay News Amsterdam*, *Gay Krant* and the *Gay Map of Amsterdam*, available at almost all gay venues. Make sure to stop by the city's gay tourist office, the Pink Point of Presence on Westermarkt, for all your needs.

TELEVISION AND RADIO
MVS Radio (103.8) offers weekly gay programming on Sunday evenings, while Dutch television serves its gay viewers with some bad cable access programmes on Monday evenings on local Amsterdam TV.

COMMUNICATIONS

Cyber cafés are plentiful. The biggest and the best of them is Easyeverything located on the Damrak and at Reguliersbreestraat 22. It is open 24 hours.

The postal service is highly efficient. You can spot a postbox by looking for the postal service logo (white letters on a red strip).

Flex that plastic

Stamps can be purchased from tobacconists or at any post office.

MAIN POST OFFICE
ℹ️ Singel 250 |✉️ 556-3311
|🕐 9am–6pm Mon–Wed & Fri; 9am–8pm Thu; 10am–1.30pm Sat; Closed Sun
|🚊 Trams 1, 2, 5, 13, 14, 17, 20

CENTRAAL STATION POST OFFICE
ℹ️ Oosterdokskade 3 |✉️ 622-8272
|🕐 8.30am–9pm Mon–Fri; 9am–noon Sat; Closed Sun |🚊 Trams 1, 2, 4, 5, 9, 13, 16, 17, 20, 24, 25

CURRENCY, CREDIT CARDS AND BANKS

As from 1 January 2002, the currency for the Netherlands became the euro. All prices in this book have been put in guilders as many of the hotels, bars and sights had not decided on their change in prices at the time of printing. The exchange rate for guilders to euros is 1€ = f 2.20.

When changing money, try to avoid the very conveniently located 24-hour kiosks whose fees and exchange rates aren't competitive. Banks and bureaux de change are usually better, but their commission fees vary.

AMERICAN EXPRESS
ℹ️ Damrak 66 |✉️ 504-8777
|🕐 9am–5pm Mon–Fri; 9am–noon Sat; Closed Sun |🚊 Trams 4, 9, 14, 16, 20, 24, 25

THOMAS COOK
ℹ️ Dam 23–25 (also at Leidseplein 31A)
|✉️ 625-0922 (626-7000)

🕐 9am–7.30pm Mon–Sat;
10am–7.30pm Sun

🚊 Trams 4, 9, 14, 16, 20, 24, 25

CREDIT CARD KEY
Amex = American Express
DC = Diners Club
M = MasterCard
V = Visa

OPENING HOURS

Traditional opening times for shops, banks and other services are 1–6pm Monday, 9am–6pm Tuesday–Wednesday and Friday, 9am–9pm Thursday, and 9am–5pm Saturday. Many businesses in the city centre now open on Sunday noon–5pm.

Banks usually open 9am–4pm Monday–Friday. Bars and clubs generally open Sunday–Thursday 11am–1am, Friday and Saturday until 2am. Restaurants are usually open noon–3pm and 5–10pm. Many restaurants close on Sunday and Monday. Museums are open daily 10am–6pm. Some of the smaller ones may close on Monday.

PUBLIC HOLIDAYS AND FESTIVALS

Public Holidays fall on New Year's Day, Good Friday, Easter Sunday, Easter Monday, Queen's Day (30 April), Remembrance Day (4 May), Liberation Day (5 May), Ascension Day, Whit (Pentecost) Sunday and Monday, Christmas Day and Boxing Day.

All government buildings, banks and offices will be closed. Shops

may open for limited periods and transport will be reduced to a Sunday service.

TIME

Amsterdam is on Central European Time, one hour ahead of GMT (Greenwich Mean Time).

ELECTRICITY

Dutch voltage is 220, 50-cycle AC. British appliances should be compatible but will require an adaptor. Visitors from North America will need to convert their electrical goods or purchase a transformer. Dutch sockets, using a two-pin continental plug, are much bigger than American ones.

TIPPING

Tipping is common in Amsterdam, with service charges often added to your bill. Check the receipt carefully before shelling out any additional funds. One particular Amsterdam quirk is the tradition of tipping club doormen. You will never be let into a club again unless you hand over at least f10.

A photo opportunity at every turn

INDEX

INDEX

NOTEBOOK

CONTACT LIST

Name

Address

Tel

Fax

email

Name

Address

Tel

Fax

email

Name

Address

Tel

Fax

email

Name

Address

Tel

Fax

email

Name

Address

Tel

Fax

email

Name

Address

Tel

Fax

email

CONTACT LIST

Name
Address

Tel
Fax
email

Name
Address

Tel
Fax
email

Name
Address

Tel
Fax
email

Name
Address

Tel
Fax
email

Name
Address

Tel
Fax
email

Name
Address

Tel
Fax
email

CONTACT LIST

Name _____   Name _____

Address _____   Address _____

_____   _____

_____   _____

Tel _____   Tel _____

Fax _____   Fax _____

email _____   email _____

Name _____   Name _____

Address _____   Address _____

_____   _____

_____   _____

Tel _____   Tel _____

Fax _____   Fax _____

email _____   email _____

Name _____   Name _____

Address _____   Address _____

_____   _____

_____   _____

Tel _____   Tel _____

Fax _____   Fax _____

email _____   email _____

Fill in details of your favourite restaurants below . . .
Tell us about them by logging on to **www.outaround.com**

Restaurant _____

Contact Details _____

Comments _____

_____

_____

_____

Restaurant _____

Contact Details _____

Comments _____

_____

_____

_____

Restaurant _____

Contact Details _____

Comments _____

_____

_____

_____

My Top Restaurants

MY TOP BARS

My Top Bars

Fill in details of your favourite bars below . . .
Tell us about them by logging on to **www.outaround.com**

Bar _____

Contact Details _____

Comments _____
_____
_____
_____
_____

Bar _____

Contact Details _____

Comments _____
_____
_____
_____
_____

Bar _____

Contact Details _____

Comments _____
_____
_____
_____
_____

Fill in details of your favourite clubs below . . .
Tell us about them by logging on to **www.outaround.com**

Club

Contact Details

Comments

Club

Contact Details

Comments

Club

Contact Details

Comments

AMSTERDAM

LONDON

MIAMI

NEW YORK

PARIS

SAN FRANCISCO

Please help us update future editions by taking part in our reader survey. Every returned form will be acknowledged and to show our appreciation we will send you a voucher entitling you to £1 off your next Out Around guide or any other Thomas Cook guidebook ordered direct from Thomas Cook Publishing. Just take a few minutes to complete this form and return it to us.

Alternatively you can visit www.outaround.com and email us the answers to the questions using the numbers given below.

We'd also be glad to hear of your comments, updates or recommendations on places we cover or you think that we ought to cover.

1   Which Out Around guide did you purchase?

2   Have you purchased other Out Around guides in the series?

☐ Yes ☐ No   If Yes, please specify

3   Which of the following tempted you into buying your Out Around guide. (Please tick as appropriate)

☐ The price
☐ The rainbow spine
☐ The cover
☐ The fact it was a dedicated gay travel guide
☐ Other

4   Please rate the following features of your 'Out Around guide' for their value to you (circle VU for 'very useful', U for 'useful', NU for 'little or no use')

'A Day Out' features	VU	U	NU
Top Sights	VU	U	NU
Top restaurants and cafés and listings	VU	U	NU
Top shops and listings	VU	U	NU
Top hotels and listings	VU	U	NU
Top clubs and bars and listings	VU	U	NU
Theatre and music venues	VU	U	NU
Gyms and sauna choices	VU	U	NU
Practical information	VU	U	NU

FEEDBACK FORM

Feedback Form

5 How did you book your holiday?

☐ Package deal
☐ Package deal through a gay-specific tour operator
☐ Flight only
☐ Accommodation only
☐ Flight and accommodation booked separately

6 How many people are travelling in your party?

7 Which other cities do you intend to/have travelled to in the next/past 12 months?

Amsterdam	Yes ☐	No ☐
London	Yes ☐	No ☐
Miami	Yes ☐	No ☐
New York	Yes ☐	No ☐
Paris	Yes ☐	No ☐
San Francisco	Yes ☐	No ☐
Other (please specify)		

8 Please tell us about any features that in your opinion could be changed, improved, or added in future editions of the book, or any other comments you would like to make concerning the book:

_____

_____

_____

_____

_____

From time to time we send our readers details of new titles or special offers. Please tick here if you wish your name to be held on our mailing list (Note: our mailing list is never sold to other companies). ☐

Please detach or photocopy this page and send it to: The Editor, Out Around, Thomas Cook Publishing, PO Box 227, The Thomas Cook Business Park, Peterborough PE3 8XX, United Kingdom.

9 Your age category
☐ under 21 ☐ 21-30 ☐ 31-40 ☐ 41-50 ☐ 51+

First name (or initials)

Last name

Your full address (Please include postal or zip code)

_____

_____

Your daytime telephone number:

_____